BRISTOL CITY

MATCH

OF MY LIFE

BRISTOL CITY
MATCH
OF MY LIFE

NEIL PALMER

**FOREWORD BY
JONATHAN PEARCE**

First published by Pitch Publishing, 2019

Pitch Publishing
A2 Yeoman Gate
Yeoman Way
Worthing
Sussex
BN13 3QZ
www.pitchpublishing.co.uk
info@pitchpublishing.co.uk

ISBN 978 1 78531 548 0

Typesetting and origination by Pitch Publishing
Printed and bound in India by Replika Press Pvt. Ltd.

CONTENTS

Author

Neil Palmer is a freelance sports writer based in Bristol, is married and has two grown-up children. He has written for various sports websites and magazines. *Bristol City: Match of my Life* is Neil's ninth book to date; others have included the popular *Derby Days* series featuring the Bristol and Welsh derbies, *Behind the Goal*, a look at Bristol City's East End, as well as the acclaimed *Trevor Ford: The Authorised Biography*, the story of Welsh football maverick Trevor Ford published in 2016.

Acknowledgements

Writing a book can be a very lonely task but at some point you need a team around you that can turn the initial enthusiasm for an idea from the page into something tangible that people will enjoy. There have been many people who have helped me produce this book along the way and, if I'm honest, this quick thank you will never really make up for how much I will be indebted to them.

I want to thank my wife Sally who can be relied upon to give me support and advice, not only during the book writing process, but through life itself – without her I would be lost – and my family and friends, again for their support in all my projects. A huge thank you to Paul and Jane Camillin and their wonderful team at Pitch Publishing for giving me the opportunity to write this book. I would also like to thank Barry Tackle, David Woods, Sean Donnelly and Wayne Hadley and his team at ConciergeUK for providing me with information and help that made the research for the book easier – this also applies to the wonderful staff at Bristol Central Library, which became my second home for a couple of months. Also a massive thank you to Dave Barton and all his staff at Bristol City Football Club, who were incredibly supportive regarding the project. Thanks must also go to lifelong City fan Jonathan Pearce for taking the time to provide me with a foreword. This book would obviously not exist without the wonderful memories from the players and again I will always be in their debt for they gave me that one priceless commodity which was their time, and listening to their stories is something I will treasure for the rest of my life; they were heroes and legends for Bristol City during their careers and they have continued to be ever since.

Neil Palmer

Introduction

It is safe to say that throughout Bristol City's 121-year history the club from the red half of Bristol has never really set the football world alight.

Yet for supporters of this great club they know all about the highs and lows of supporting their local side. For City are amongst a rare set of clubs that have spent time in all four divisions. They have experienced the euphoria of four years in the top flight of English football during the seventies under manager Alan Dicks, whilst also going through the subsequent collapse on and off the pitch during the 1980s as the club fell through the divisions, the club at that time coming within 20 minutes of going out of business, before eight players on long contracts ripped them up and saved the club.

Since those days the club has had various promotions and relegations through the lower divisions, yet today they find themselves in the Championship and banging on the door of the Premier League with a wealthy owner Stephen Lansdown and a young British manager in Lee Johnson, which in itself is a rarity in today's game. This combination along with a new state-of-the-art stadium which would grace any Premier League ground will hopefully get the club back into the top flight for the first time since 1980.

But what of the years that have gone before? Behind today's success is a list of City teams over the years that, like the supporters, have experienced highs and lows such as promotions, relegations, Wembley euphoria and Wembley heartache, with the odd giant-killing cup run thrown in for good measure. All those teams have thrown up fans' heroes. Ask a granddad on the terraces of his hero and he will probably tell you watching keeper Mike Gibson diving at an opponent's feet or a dazzling run from Jantzen Derrick, maybe even the perfect displays of captain Geoff Merrick or the sadness of Paul Cheesley's career being cut short when it promised so much. Any fathers will tell you of Alan Walsh's shuffle or the joy of watching Super Bobby Taylor celebrate a goal. And for today's youngsters it might have been Louis Carey reading a game like no one else or the speed and skill of Scotty Murray as he punished another defence from a perfect Brian Tinnion left-foot pass.

It has been my privilege through writing this book to have met and spoken to many of the legends throughout Bristol City's past. It has been an honour to spend time with them and particularly notice how the game has changed for the footballer over the years. Whether it's Mike Gibson making sure he finishes his apprenticeship before he can even think of becoming a footballer or Lee Johnson dealing with foreign agents and players in a world where an average player commands in a week what some fans earn in a year, one thing has come through all these players' stories and that is of men who cared about wearing the red shirt of Bristol City. Many were local lads but also many knew nothing about the club before they signed for the Robins but something about it stayed inside them. I certainly found this to be true when I tracked people down for their contribution to the book and to a man their reply was 'Of course I will do it – I love the club'. Hopefully the memories of these legends of Ashton Gate will bring back some memories for you the reader and I hope it will confirm that we were all in this together.

Neil Palmer

Foreword

How to choose the 'Match of my Life' from years of watching the team that simply was my life for so many years? A near impossible task for me I'm afraid.

I still remember the thrill of my first ever game. Saturday, 14 September 1968. Derby County with their up and coming young manager Brian Clough. My dad and I stood behind the dugouts on the terrace in front of the main stand.

The programme, costing one shilling, had a photo of keeper Mike Gibson rising high to catch a ball on its front page with Bobby Kellard looking on. I still have it to this day. A little worn around the edges. Tattered and torn: it's a little like a life supporting Bristol City FC!

The team on page three reads: Mike Gibson; Trevor Jacobs, Jack Connor, Gordon Parr, Alec Briggs; Chris Crowe, Ken Wimshurst, Kellard, Gerry Sharpe; John Galley and my first footballing pin-up boy, of course, Chris Garland.

It finished 0–0. Clough called me 'a disgrace' for swearing and banging on the Derby dugout roof. I was innocent! It was the big-un from 'Artcliffe' stood next to me. They were the only words the great man ever spoke to me! I'll never forget it.

Alan Dicks was a neighbour. I adored him. Dad and I started working for the club televising the games for tactical purposes. We covered every game for eight years until I started work for BBC Radio Bristol. The players adopted us as part of the team it seemed to me. Great days as I was growing up.

A trip to cavernous Molineux and historic Wolves in the cup. Didn't John Emmanuel have to go in goal? Being around the promotion-winning team as it grew – wonderful!

Hat-tricks for big Paul Cheesley and Tom Ritchie in the games against York stick in the mind. Clive Whitehead's promotion winner against Portsmouth! Sipping champagne with Don Gillies from a policeman's helmet on the steps outside the directors' room long after the full-time whistle.

Cheesley climbing as high as the Highbury floodlights to head home on the opening day of First Division football at Arsenal. Ashton Gate packed to the rafters for that late season drama against Liverpool. The final match at Coventry. God what drama! Didn't we stop at the Red Lion in Stratford on the way home to get drunk? I was underage. No one cared.

I loved those players. I still do. There are so many games and magical memories for me and I will love reading those of the players who have helped Neil on the book.

But I have to finish on the one game I have picked. Leeds in the 1974 FA Cup fifth round. My bedroom walls were covered with Leeds and City pictures. To that moment my allegiance was divided. Eddie Gray was one of my all-time favourite players. Bremner, Giles, Clarke. I worshipped them until the draw. Then my mind was clear. It was City all the way even though no one gave them a chance.

Don Revie's men were unbeaten after 29 games at the top of the First Division. Nine points clear of second-placed Liverpool. City were scuffling along in the Second Division.

But at Ashton Gate on the Saturday my all-time football hero became a star. Gerry Gow, a friend and mentor, dumped Bremner and Giles on their backsides in the opening exchanges. Bremner did score from 25 yards but Gerry kept scowling, prowling and terrorising.

I'll never forget Gerry snapping into a tackle and sending a lovely ball through for Keith Fear's wonderful lob to earn the replay. I was so excited I leapt off the TV gantry. A BBC cameraman clutched my collar, saved me and inflicted years of JP commentary on all of you.

I can still see Dave Harvey's save of a lifetime to claw out a Don Gillies header and deny City a famous win.

On the Tuesday at Elland Road, though, our 'Flying Scotsman' wasn't to be denied again.

With the government enforcing the three-day week and cutting power due to industrial action by the miners, the replay had to be played in the afternoon.

There were 47,182 though. The highest crowd of the season. The pitch was soft and sandy. The tackles from Geoff Merrick and 18-year-old Gary Collier were rock hard. Ray Cashley made bold saves. Lorimer hit the post.

Seventy-three minutes in Gerry robbed Bremner yet again, found Keith with a long pass; the lovely, grumpy, maverick forward brilliantly fed Donny who held off our soon to be idolised Norman Hunter and fired home the greatest goal of his career. From Scottish Merchant Navy deckhand to Bristol City legend!

I was privileged to sit in the dressing room afterwards between that old walrus Ernie Hunt and my superman Gerry. I was in wonderland.

Someone said Bill Shankly was outside. City had been drawn to play Liverpool in the quarter-final.

'Go and talk to him,' said Alan Dicks. 'Tell him you are from Bristol City. He loves talking football.'

And so I did. He was stood by his car waiting for the traffic to clear. Terrified, I made the approach. Ecstatically, I listened as he heaped praise on Gerry. Chastened, I departed for the dressing room again as he warned 'Ye've nae chance against us laddie!' I can hear his growl now.

He did beat us in the next round. It didn't matter. Because I had cried my tears of joy sitting alongside my heroes in that dressing room. The elation of promotion of course was to come and all those memories. But Elland Road that day was the stuff of legend. My team had beaten the best in the land and I had been made to feel very much a part of it.

I still love all of those players to this day. Critics say I shouldn't openly declare my allegiance because of my job. I don't care who knows. Even to this day as I approach a Premier League commentary position you will hear me singing 'Ee's Yur … ee's there … he's every f***ing where … Gerry Gow … Gerry Gow'.

A life supporting a football club. The hope and despair. The joy and failure. All of life wrapped up in that red shirt.

Well done to Neil. This is a superb collection. Enjoy!

Jonathan Pearce

The Players

LOUIS CAREY

Louis Carey

Louis Carey was certainly 'one of our own'. The young defender watched the club from the terraces and signed his first professional contract with City in 1995. A loyal and honest servant of the club, Carey holds the record for the number of appearances in the red shirt. His 646 games for the club puts him ahead of the great John Atyeo and it's truly a record that will take a long time to be beaten in the modern game. This versatile, quality defender has had a love affair with the club since the age of ten, but like many love affairs they sometimes hit a rocky patch and that happened to Louis after the team's shambolic display against Brighton in the League One play-off final defeat at Cardiff's Millennium Stadium in 2004. Louis's contract was up and there was no agreement from the club on renewing it, so Carey left and joined Peter Reid at Coventry City. There was an outcry from the supporters when the likeable Bristolian left but no surprise six months later when the two kissed and made up so Carey could return to the club, incidentally taking a pay cut to come back to Ashton Gate. Carey went from strength to strength as an inspirational captain under various managers. A real student of the game, he finally hung up his boots in 2015.

Bristol City 2 Crystal Palace 1 (AET)
Football League Championship play-off
semi-final second leg
13 May 2008
Ashton Gate

Bristol City: Basso, Orr, McCombe, Carey, McAllister, Noble, Carle, Elliott, McIndoe, Trundle, Adebola. Subs: Weale, Byfield, Fontaine, Johnson, Sproule.

Goals: Trundle, McIndoe.

My time at Bristol City is littered with games that stick in my mind. My debut was really special. I had been with the reserves playing Ipswich Town at Clevedon Town's ground and I was taken off with about half an hour to go. To say I was angry was an understatement, but little did I know I would then be travelling up with the first team to play York City. I travelled on the coach and Joe Jordan was manager. I couldn't believe it when my name was read out on the team sheet. That Bristol City dressing room I joined at the tender age of 18 was full of experienced pros like Mark Shail, David Nugent, Brian Tinnion, Gary Owers and Rob Edwards. I remember I got no special treatment, rightly so, and they just let me deal with the nerves in my own way which was great. The only instruction I had was how we would play and what balls to put up to the front lads. I stood in the tunnel before coming out and, although there were only about 3,000 fans at York, the noise and the effect it had on me made it feel like it was 300,000. I never stopped getting that feeling when I walked out for any match for City; it was like a pure shot of adrenalin.

There were also games against Watford the year we won promotion with John Ward that are high on my list, along with games against local rivals Bristol Rovers which were always great affairs for us and the fans. I also recall the home leg of the play-off semi-final against Hartlepool United under manager Danny Wilson. That game had the whole of Ashton Gate buzzing; I could genuinely feel the stadium shaking.

But when I look back on my career I have to say the one 'Match of my Life' that I will take away from my time at the club has to be the Championship play-off semi-final second leg against Crystal Palace at Ashton Gate. We had a phenomenal season that year; we were the surprise package of the league after coming up straight from Division One the previous year. In reality we just thought we could consolidate in our first year but the atmosphere Gary Johnson and his staff created around the place was awesome.

I had a lot of time for Gary as a manager; he had a drive and a buzz for football. I know he wasn't everybody's cup of tea but I liked his dry sense of humour and I could see that now and again he would drop bombs on players and see how they reacted. If you were the type of player who threw your toys out of the pram you were not what he needed when things got tough. Trouble was, there were some players who couldn't see that about him.

Towards the end of the season we had lost that consistency that we showed all through the campaign. We were the type of side that you could not write off. If we were 1–0 down with minutes to go we would make it 1–1, and if it was 1–1 with minutes to go invariably we would pull out a winner. But of late, leading into the Palace games, we had lost a few times and critics were starting to question us. In the camp we were strong and resolute and that eventually pulled us through.

The first leg play-off semi at Selhurst Park was a real rollercoaster in terms of emotion. There was not much between either of us in the first half as it ended 0–0. In the second half again it was chances at both ends before the game exploded into life. Lee Trundle was fouled on the edge of the box and we had a free kick. Noble and McIndoe stood over it and I drifted into the melee of players in the box. We knew what we were going to do as we had done it on the training pitch a million times. Noble pushed it to McIndoe and at that moment I lost my marker, the ball was passed to me and I just hit it into the corner for my first goal of the season. It was incredible. The lads just piled on me and the bench was in uproar. We laughed about it working and there was no greater feeling than that moment. We were in control but then they pushed defender Fonte up front to try and cause us problems and he did. All of a sudden a ball was played up front, I lost my footing in a tackle with him and I brought him down in the box. Referee Howard Webb pointed to the spot and I felt gutted not only for me but for the lads. They stuck the penalty home and got on top with us clinging on to stay in the game. With that, Noble produced a piece of genius and struck a ball from outside the box that the keeper had no chance with. It completely silenced the home fans and gave us the lead going into the second leg at Ashton Gate.

The game at Ashton Gate still gives me goosebumps today. It was a fabulous, warm evening with the sun just going down, and a combination of the dark blue sky along with the sea of red and white the fans had produced made the ground look really special. I remember the warm-up and due to the atmosphere and the feeling I was getting from the fans I had never been so relaxed before a game in my life. Gary was the same as he spoke to us before we went out. He told us that we could do it and to just show them what we were made of. As I stood in the tunnel I could see the fans at the old East End and the pitch looked like a lovely lush green carpet. Everything was perfect, and I got that natural shot of adrenalin that I always got walking out in a red shirt. As we got on to the pitch the noise was deafening and credit to those fans, they were as up for it as we were.

We had done our homework on them and knew Neil Warnock had a great record when it came to play-offs, so Gary and his coaching team had to be tactically astute which they certainly were. We had studied their front three of Sinclair, who was young and quick, Clinton Morrison, who had been there and done it, and another youngster Scannell, who again was quick. We knew we had to stop them from playing and getting the ball. We got at them right from the off and their defender cleared an Elliott header off their line within the opening few minutes which gave the fans a massive buzz. It was pretty much nip and tuck to start with but then after about 25 minutes they played a long ball into the box and there was a mix-up between Basso in our goal and McCombe and the result was that their midfielder Watson put them 1–0 up and now the tie was level. It certainly silenced the crowd and you could feel the nervousness going right around the ground. We still had the belief but we were really under the cosh and almost hanging on as they came right at us. Fortunately the referee blew for half-time and we could go and regroup. In the dressing room Gary was calm and level-headed; this was no time for balling anybody out. He just told us we would be okay and to remember the first leg. He tweaked a few things like moving Noble inside and then off we went for the second half.

Fair play to the crowd – they got behind us from the kick-off and again it was a very close game. I remember the floodlights were on now and Ashton Gate under floodlights is a very special place, particularly when there is something on the game and there was no bigger prize than the chance to get to Wembley. The game was really even but then with about 20 minutes to go Palace put a long throw into the box and Nick Carle brought a Palace player down so the ref gave a penalty. We were on the floor; this was it, possibly the end of our season. I, like the rest of the lads, stood there as Watson stepped up to take it in front of the East End that housed both our fans and theirs. As he struck it Basso guessed the right way and flicked it on to the post. I think in that moment Palace were finished and we just stepped up a gear. The noise from the crowd was as if we had scored and they felt the same as us that this could be our night and our season wasn't ending tonight.

When the game went to extra time we could see that the Palace players were finished and Gary told us as much before it started. It was an incredible night and when Trunds scored and then McIndoe's fabulous strike put us 2–1 up the joy was immense; my heart was bursting with excitement. We were all in it together and we refused to be beaten which is how we had been all season. When the whistle blew and the crowd came on the pitch, I remember thinking nights like this and with a group of players like this are why you go and play football. We were immense that night and our fitness levels in extra time were extraordinary. The dressing room after was incredible but we realised that we had only done half a job and tonight was pointless if we were going to get beat at Wembley.

The play-off final against Hull City was another milestone in my career. I have played in quite a few important games over the years for City and, in all honesty, for a few of them we just never turned up as a side, but at Wembley I never felt that. Looking back at the game, we had so many chances to win it over the 90 minutes that I am still astonished that we didn't. The defeat was incredibly hard to take. I wanted to do what Geoff Merrick had done in the 1970s: take my local club all the way to the top flight but it was not to be. I know Gary was deeply upset and he felt some of the lads had let him down, but I just felt certain players may have let themselves down, and whether it was nerves or we just froze, the bottom line was that it was just not meant to be. After the game I took a long hard look at my own performance and I asked myself, could I have done more? No. Did I give it everything I had? Yes. So as long as I could answer those questions honestly I would just have to put it to bed and think about that fantastic season where we came so close.

My career continued at the club but we certainly never reached those dizzy heights again. Then, when Steve Cotterill was in charge, I got a call to his office and he told me he was letting me go. I was upset as I thought I could have had another year with the club and maybe be a help to the youngsters coming through, but I understood football and to be fair Steve was good as gold about it. I see him now and then and he always says he felt terrible doing that to me but we both know it's part of the game.

I thought long and hard about what to do next and to be honest I had had enough of the backstabbing and bullshit that went with the game, so I took a year off and did some voluntary work at a couple of charities that I was involved in. Although I had a few offers I had had enough of the game during that time and the charity work made me focus on things that were important in life. During my time away I had calls from a mate to come and coach the kids at Southampton Academy, but I kept putting him off. I was also asked time and time again by local landlord and City nut Sean Donnelly to come and play for his side, the Three Lions. In the end I did and turned out with the likes of Scott Murray and Colin Cramb. I loved it – it was just lads getting together to play local football on a Sunday with terrible pitches and terrible facilities but we had such a laugh that it really rejuvenated my love of the game. I also played eight games for Shepton Mallett as a favour to a mate of mine who I had met through the charity work. In the end I took up the offer to coach at Southampton Academy and I can honestly say it has been incredible and really worthwhile, working with youngsters on their hopeful journeys to become professional footballers.

Looking back, I am very proud to have captained my boyhood team and to hold the record for number of appearances – beating John Atyeo is something I will always cherish. I still go back to the club now and then and I get a great reception as I also do when I am turning out for the Lions in local football. In the future I would love to be a manager but the way the game is now it's a very difficult road to even get considered for any job, so we will see. I have enjoyed looking back and I will never forget that lovely warm night at Ashton Gate when a team that were mates refused to be beaten.

Paul Cheesley

To the fans who stood on the terraces during the seventies there was only one hero and that was Paul Cheesley. Born in Bristol, this talented striker rejected both Bristol clubs as a youngster and it was at Norwich City that he would gain his first taste of first-team football. City always kept tabs on the one that got away and in 1973 manager Alan Dicks paid Norwich £30,000 to bring the striker home. Paul excelled in the young City side that Dicks was putting together and his powerful shot with either foot and great timing in the air turned him into a potent striker who became the talisman for City's famous promotion to Division One in 1976. With promotion Paul exploded on to the football scene, getting the winner in a 1–0 victory over Arsenal at Highbury in City's first game in the top flight. Three days after the euphoria of the win Cheesley twisted his knee in a game against Stoke City after a collision with Stoke keeper Peter Shilton. Months of operations followed but Paul was lost to league football forever. What he could have achieved in the game will keep fans talking forever but he did enough for City fans to love him forever.

Sunderland 1 Bristol City 1
Football League Second Division
23 March 1976
Roker Park

Bristol City: Cashley, Sweeney, Drysdale, Gow, Collier, Merrick, Tainton, Ritchie, Gillies, Cheesley, Whitehead. Sub: Mann.

Goal: Sweeney.

Although my career was relatively short I have no problem recalling some of the games during it. I was a Bristol lad who went away to make his name in the game. Yes, I had both Bristol City and Bristol Rovers after my signature when I was 14 but they both told me that if I signed I couldn't play football with my mates in the local team. So incredibly I told them no and just wrote off to a couple of other teams to see if they would give me a chance. Looking back, I don't know if it was confidence or stupidity, but it worked and I ended up getting spotted by Norwich City.

I enjoyed my time there and I liked working with their legendary manager Ron Saunders. Ron had quite a fearsome reputation in the game for being a bit of a dour character but I liked the fact that he was very much a 'man's man' who wouldn't bullshit you and told you how things were. Ron gave me my start in the game and in particular my debut against Manchester United at Old Trafford which was a real thrill for me. I also got my first league goal which was against Liverpool, so it wasn't a bad start for me. Ron stayed at the club a few years before moving on to Aston Villa where he did brilliantly. New man John Bond was okay but the club were starting to get offers for me and Bond was happy to cash in I think.

One of those offers was from my hometown club of Bristol City and their relatively new young manager Alan Dicks, who was in the process of building a side. Dicks ended up getting my signature for £30,000 which was still a lot of money back then ... I was sad to leave Norwich as the club and supporters had been good to me but it was great to come back to Bristol. Dicks was putting together a new side whilst also slowly dismantling the old one. The dressing room I joined had players like Len Bond, Ernie Hunt, Geoff Merrick and Gerry Sweeney, so it was really the nucleus of lads that would go on and win promotion some three years later. I remember my debut which was at home to Leyton Orient – we lost 2–0 due to two own goals which was ridiculous at the time. I always let my feelings be known to Alan Dicks and the players if I thought things were not right and I know a lot of them were not particularly impressed or used to that sort of honesty, but I was brought up being with Ron Saunders and I suppose that certain bluntness he had rubbed off at times. I remember having full-on rows with Dicksy, especially when he had a go at me for not chasing full-backs back down the pitch. I used to say 'Why did you buy me?'

I know I will forever be linked with one of Bristol City's greatest footballing days: that incredible win at Highbury against Arsenal in our first game in the top flight. I remember it like it was yesterday, with the boiling hot sun beating down on us and all those incredible supporters who made the trip up the M4 to support us. When I close my eyes I can still see the ball coming in from Clive Whitehead and me just hanging in the air waiting to head it into the corner. I know I gave poor old David O'Leary a real runaround that afternoon and, looking back, the Arsenal team had some great players in it like Alan Ball, John Radford, Pat Rice, George Armstrong and, of course, Malcolm Macdonald, who had just signed for a British transfer record of £330,000. The celebrations after were incredible. In the match, I lost about half a stone in weight due to sweating but I certainly put it back on in the players' bar afterwards.

As I said, it was a game that will always be linked with me, but the one game I have to pick for 'Match of my Life' was the game against Sunderland in the promotion season, not only for what was happening to me but for the effort the lads showed in that particular game. It was a defining match that made us realise that we could actually gain promotion with the players we had. For me the time at Bristol City was going brilliantly. I had forged a great partnership up front with Tom Ritchie and we were both banging in the goals and getting lots of attention. With us flying high in the table we knew we were not that far away from finishing in the top three if we could just hold things together. I never thought of us as a team of stars, just a collective bunch of lads that would go through walls for each other. We had shown incredible resolution after going to West Brom, who were also chasing promotion, and winning 1–0 with a 13-pass Gerry Sweeney goal after defending for 80-odd minutes. That result also made the media stand up and think that maybe Bristol City could be the dark horses this year. After a home draw against Fulham, next we were away at leaders Sunderland in a game that could well decide the title even though none of us were promoted that day.

In the build-up to the game I received a letter from the Football Association. It said that due to my recent performances for Bristol City I had been invited by England manager Don Revie to train at Lilleshall with the England side and play for the under-23s against Hungary at Old Trafford the following evening. I was deeply proud and also in turmoil as the following evening was the same night that City were due to play Sunderland at Roker Park. I walked around Ashton Gate for what seemed an age, thinking my dilemma over and over. This was to be a pivotal game in Bristol City's season but also this was a chance to get an England cap and international recognition. Every time I came up with a solution I changed my mind. In the end I decided that I would give the letter to captain Geoff Merrick and get him to read it out in front of the lads. If they didn't appear pleased that I had been recognised or tried to take the mick then I would go to the England setup. If, however, they were supportive and thought it was well deserved then that was enough for me and I would stay and fight for the cause against Sunderland. Geoff read it out and to a man they all clapped and cheered and told me I deserved it, so my mind was made up and I told them I wouldn't be going and I was putting City first. I know Alan Dicks has stated that he stopped me going but that's not true – I made the decision and I stuck to it.

We were quietly confident going up to Sunderland. I had put any thoughts of England completely out of my mind and my sole task was for us to try and get something out of what would be a difficult game. We went up to the north-east a couple of days before and stayed on the coast in a place called Seaburn. It was really relaxing; we did a bit of training and walked along the beach a few times and to be honest the England call-up thing was furthest from my mind. Alan Dicks did his homework and briefed us all. We knew it would be a tough ask as they were top of the league and only three years previous they had won the FA Cup after beating Leeds United at Wembley. In the press, many were talking about this being a championship decider but we just wanted to get something out of the game. There were 40,000 crammed into Roker Park that night and the atmosphere was incredible. Alan's team talk was just the usual chat about winning your personal battles and making sure we got hold of the midfield in order to run the game. Me and Tom Ritchie had a little chat regarding how we were going to play their back two and off we went.

As you would expect, the game was very much nip and tuck with not many chances at either end. I had a wallop from the Sunderland centre-back early on which hurt like hell so he certainly did his job in letting me know he was there. We started to play our normal game and opened them up a bit. I remember we should have had a stonewall penalty when Tom was pushed in the box by Sunderland defender Joe Bolton but the ref just waved it away. Minutes later I was also hauled to the ground by Bobby Moncur but our claims for a penalty fell on deaf ears. We went in at half-time level although we were livid with the referee and I remember Alan Dicks having a go at him in the tunnel on the way to the changing rooms. The changing room was just a noise of players calling the ref every name under the sun and it seemed everybody was having their say about the decisions, before Geoff Merrick and Alan Dicks shouted for us to calm down and just get on with things. Alan told us a goal would come and if we got one it would silence the fans in the second half.

With the start of the second half we put together a move that many thought was our goal of the season. Brian Drysdale, Gerry Gow and Tom Ritchie linked up cleverly and I flicked the ball sideways to Brian, who pulled the ball back to Gerry Sweeney and he volleyed the ball into the net. It stunned the Roker Park faithful and it was another important goal from Gerry on the way to our promotion. We were playing some incredible football and you could have heard a pin drop in the ground as it looked like we would be the first team to win at Roker for 14 months. But one lack of concentration let them in. A ball over the top was left by Gary Collier and Sunderland's Bobby Kerr stole in to head the ball home and give them some much-needed confidence. We weathered the initial onslaught and I came off with about four minutes to go due to the knock

I had early on in the game. I remember being sat in the dugout desperate for the ref to blow his whistle. In the end a 1–1 draw was a fair result. We had probably played the best we had all season. In goal, Cash was incredible, as were the back four, especially Geoff Merrick who was my man of the match that night, and the midfield lads like Gerry Gow and Trevor Tainton won everything. We were disappointed not to win but we knew that promotion was very much on the cards now. I think that's why the game sticks in my mind so much as we really played like a team that night and we showed what we were capable of. It epitomised the philosophy of what was running through the club at that time, about how we were all there for each other no matter what and that spirit is what got us promotion weeks later.

After the game on the way home I couldn't help but look at the press report from the England game. They had won 3–1. I remember the team had a few top players in it like Ray Wilkins, Steve Coppell, Stuart Pearson, Alan Kennedy and Jimmy Case. I was gutted but City's performance made up for it and I thought I'm going nowhere so they will come again. Unfortunately that was not to be.

We clinched promotion with a 1–0 win at home to Portsmouth on what again was a special night for the club although we were terrible that night due to nerves more than anything. The win got us up with Sunderland who were champions and West Brom who finished behind us in third place. Our preseason was great and we were raring to go in the top flight. The Arsenal win gave us a start we could only dream about and we looked to keep the momentum going the following Tuesday night at home to Stoke City in what turned out to be another game that I will always be linked with.

I had tweaked my knee in the game against Sunderland and I knew it hurt but didn't really give it much thought. Anyway, I went up for a ball with Stoke City keeper Peter Shilton and I fell awkwardly. The pain was unbearable and I knew it wasn't good. I got stretchered off and that's when the nightmare began. To say the club didn't handle the whole situation very well is an understatement. I worked really hard on the knee although at the time nobody seemed to know what the problem was. I spent weeks upon weeks on my own running up and down the Dolman Stand in a bid to try and strengthen it. There was a light at the end of the tunnel and it was the home game with Birmingham City which I got myself in contention for. I made the team which was a massive thing for me considering I had been out for nine weeks.

In the end I came through the game unscathed which considering how my game was all about putting yourself about was a minor miracle. I knew, though, that the knee was still not right. We lost the game 1–0 and things didn't really help when manager Alan Dicks went to the local paper and said that 'Cheesley just has to play through the pain barrier'. I was livid as it implied the injury was all in my head. I went to the club and locked

myself, Alan Dicks and his assistant Ken Wimshurst
in an office determined I was not going to leave until I
had it out with them. Alan just tried to cover his arse,
saying that wasn't what he meant and how he had been
misquoted, and poor old Ken just looked shell-shocked
but I was still livid. I also asked the *Bristol Evening Post*
to retract the article as I thought it was a scandalous
piece of journalism and I expected more from them but
they never changed it. In the end the club agreed for
me to see a specialist in Harley Street which you would
have thought would have been the first thing they would
have done.

So unbelievably I got injured in August and had
my first X-ray on the knee in October. The specialist,
a guy called Ian Williams, told me that I should not
have been running up and down the stands with it as
it made it worse. I had damaged both ligaments and
all the surrounding cartilage of the knee. In total I had
36 weeks of rehab on it but as far as Mr Williams was
concerned he didn't think I would play again. With
my contract already running down I was summoned
to the boardroom where there were Alan Dicks, all
the directors, the club doctor and the physio. The club
said that they were not taking the option on me and
were not offering me any type of deal. I told them I
would get fit and play next season for half my money
but they declined. To add insult to injury, I was valued
at my height at around £250,000, but the club had
only insured me for £50,000, and I was entitled to a

percentage of that which turned out to be just under £10,000 plus a testimonial.

When I look back on that time I was just fodder really and the club just disregarded me and treated me shockingly in terms of helping me with the injury. I always felt that I just wasn't looked after. I had the testimonial which was against my old club Norwich City but the date was changed two or three times and in the end only around 4,000 fans turned up for it which was sad. I found it difficult hanging up the boots in those circumstances but I still love this club and I am always proud to be asked to do the corporate hospitality on matchdays and meet all the fans, especially when they say 'You should have played for England, Paul'.

JANTZEN DERRICK

Jantzen Derrick

Jantzen Derrick was truly a star in the making when he signed for his hometown club Bristol City in 1959. This England schoolboy was pursued by many of the top clubs, but it was always going to be City for this youngster. He made his debut at Lincoln City's Sincil Bank aged 16 years and 324 days making him the youngest player ever to play for the Robins. Derrick went from strength to strength under the guidance of manager Fred Ford. There was no doubting Derrick's skill and talent but like many with his natural ability he split the Ashton Gate faithful as many saw him as inconsistent, while to others he was the talent to build the team around.

Jantzen spent 12 years at Ashton Gate, playing alongside great forwards such as John Atyeo and Brian Clark. Manager Alan Dicks released Derrick in 1971 after a brief spell on loan at Mansfield. Incredibly he was then signed by Paris Saint-Germain, becoming one of the first foreign players ever to play for the Paris club. After one season in France, Jantzen returned to his beloved Bristol where he took a job outside the game whilst playing non-league football in the area. Jantzen played 292 games for City and scored 36 goals in the process. He will always be a very special player to the Bristol City fans, even the ones he frustrated.

Tottenham Hotspur 2 Bristol City 0
FA Cup fifth round
11 March 1967
White Hart Lane

Bristol City: Gibson, Ford, Briggs, Parr, Connor, Low, Derrick, Crowe, Bush, Quigley, Peters.

Bristol City have always been my club and when I look back I have always thought of it as an honour to have played for them. My career gave me some fantastic memories of games and also of players I have played with and against over the years. I still live a stone's throw from Ashton Gate and when I go to games now I always get a terrific reaction from the fans and I find that really touching.

I was pursued by a whole host of clubs when I was younger; I remember Arsenal and Chelsea being very keen but it was always going to be Bristol City for me. I was picked for England Schoolboys and played in some great games, particularly against West Germany at Wembley in front of 90,000 fans and also up at Hampden Park where we turned out against Scotland in front of around 100,000, which was pretty daunting for a 15-year-old but it really did set me up in my career. I also got a hat-trick against Ireland and it could have been more as I missed a penalty as well, so I had some success at England Schoolboy level. In total I got six caps for England and I have to say they were a really good side at the time with players like Terry Venables and Peter Thompson. In fact, Terry became a really good friend over the years.

I joined the ground staff at City in 1958. I was 15 years old and that meant I was cleaning players' boots, sweeping the terraces and in the summer painting those terraces – in fact, doing just about any odd job within the club. I remember when we had to sweep the terracing,

I would always make a beeline for the large East End terrace part of the ground as you would have much more chance of picking up a few bob that the late drunken supporters had dropped on their way in.

The club at the time were in the old Second Division and managed by Peter Doherty, the former Irish international inside-right. He also managed the Irish team. Doherty was a class player in his day, winning the title with Manchester City and the FA Cup with Derby County. He had also played for Huddersfield Town and Doncaster Rovers so he had really seen and done it all. I remember him in training and you could still see that he had lost none of his skill and desire. Unfortunately Doherty decided to bring a lot of players with him from the north of England and that, combined with all the local lads in the side, made for a very fractious changing room.

I remember being asked to train with the first team which was incredible, rubbing shoulders with players like John Atyeo and Bobby Williams. When I joined them on the cinder track that ran around Ashton Gate, there were two groups of players running around the ground: the locals and the northerners. It was a very difficult situation especially for a young, impressionable 15-year-old lad. It was Doherty who gave me my debut away against Lincoln City. I remember just seeing my name on the team sheet that had been pinned to the wall in the dressing room a few days before. I was over the moon and to be honest I was really not that nervous as

I had played before huge crowds when I was playing for England Schoolboys, but, that said, I was a bit anxious about coming up against men instead of boys. The lads were great to me and they all wished me well before the game.

The match itself flew by. It ended 1–1 and I came off the pitch with a few knocks but in one piece which was the main thing. Doherty and his assistant Cliff Duffin were keen to throw me in the side at any chance they could, which was great, but I remember getting a call to play in the England youth trials but it clashed with a game against Plymouth Argyle. The club really pressured me into playing against Plymouth but I do regret not getting a chance to play in the trial. Things were coming to a head regarding the tension in the side and after a disappointing relegation to Division Three in 1960/61 Peter Doherty was sacked and physio Les Bardsley was put in charge before a replacement could be found. That replacement was found in the July in the shape of former Millwall, Charlton and Carlisle player Fred Ford.

Ford immediately got into the groups that had formed in the dressing room and started to build some team spirit. The club certainly responded and the whole atmosphere of the place seemed to change from his very arrival.

As I said, I have some really great memories of matches for City, particularly games against rivals Bristol Rovers which were always a bit tasty and really important for the fans with bragging rights up for grabs. But the game that really sticks in my mind is the FA Cup fifth round game against Tottenham Hotspur at White Hart Lane.

It was a really big game for us. We were doing okay in Division Two and Spurs were flying high in Division One with a tremendous team consisting of Pat Jennings, Dave Mackay, Alan Mullery, Terry Venables and, of course, Jimmy Greaves. We had a really good side as well back then. Mike Gibson was fantastic in goal – his bravery was exceptional. At the back we had Tony Ford and Alec Briggs who were tough full-backs; added to that were Gordon Parr and Jack Connor who were again big tough opponents for any striker. Midfield was myself, Terry Bush, Chris Crowe and Gordon Low, so we could all play a bit, and up front was Johnny Quigley and Lou Peters, so we were a match for anybody.

When the draw was made, the first thing manager Fred Ford did was tell us that we would have to watch out for Jimmy Greaves. In the build-up to the game it was touch and go whether Greaves would be fit as he was suffering from flu and had missed Spurs' last two games, but come the day he was there on the team sheet. Driving to the ground was a fantastic feeling. I had played at White Hart Lane in the Combination League but this was going to be a full house of 55,000. City took around 10,000 fans and it was incredible to see all the red and white scarves lining the route to the ground. We were real underdogs and nobody except the City fans gave us a chance. As we got off the bus the fans cheered and clapped us; it was a fantastic feeling knowing that they had all travelled to see us. We all got in the changing room and Fred told the defence to be wary of the ball over the top as Greaves would play on the shoulder of the last man and he would be off after it; one on one was his bread and butter, especially with his finishing.

As we were warming up on the pitch, my old mate Terry Venables, who was playing in midfield for Spurs, came over to me and told me that full-back Cyril Knowles was ready to kick me all over the pitch. We both laughed and I told Terry not to worry as Cyril won't get near me. The game kicked off and, with my first touch, running after me was Cyril, but I have to say I pushed the ball past him and he never caught me. I remember Spurs came right at us from the start and to be honest we were all over the place. Dave Mackay was certainly putting himself about; he caught Johnny Quigley with what looked like a fist in the first five minutes of the game after we had been awarded a free kick. We all thought he was being sent off as I'm sure the ref pointed to the tunnel but Mackay got right into his face arguing the toss and he stayed on the field. Fair play to Johnny, though, he certainly never made a meal of the challenge; in fact, I think it was only Johnny's reaction that kept Mackay on the pitch. I would love to have seen what would happen in today's game.

The lads in defence were up against it right from the off and were doing well until a ball over the top got

Greaves on his toes and he slotted the ball past Gibbo in goal. It really was classic Jimmy Greaves but to be honest Gordon Parr was doing an excellent job marking him until then; it was literally the first chance he had in the first half. We had a few chances of our own and I got down the wing to put some crosses in the box which caused them a few problems and it did my confidence the world of good. We went in at half-time 1–0 down. Fred was pleased and we had certainly given Spurs something to think about and they knew they were in a game.

In the second half, the game exploded into action. We missed an absolute sitter when Chris Crowe ran through three defenders and hit a thunderbolt that Jennings in the Spurs goal could only push out to the oncoming Terry Bush but he stuck it wide from five yards. Then I took a corner and Spurs centre-half Mike England handled in the box. Tony Ford took our penalty but Jennings saved it. We were gutted as the place erupted but then the referee blew for it to be retaken as Jennings had moved before the kick was taken. It was a real lifeline and I remember thinking maybe it could be our game. As we were ready to take the second, Chris Crowe stepped up, took the ball out of Tony Ford's hands and placed it on the spot telling Fordy that he was taking it. With that, incredibly Crowe's penalty went a good two yards wide. Chris would normally blast them but he went to place it and I think he just changed his mind at the last minute. I couldn't believe it and neither could the rest of the lads, especially Chris who just stood with his head in his hands. The Spurs fans went crazy, as they knew it had been a let-off for them. It was a real blow for us but we had to compose ourselves and keep going if we were to get anything out of the tie.

We kept going and the defence were brilliant. Gordon Parr and Jack Connor were exceptional in snuffing Greaves and Gilzean out of the game. Then with minutes left Gordon Low handled in the box and Greaves stuck home the penalty with what was his second touch of the ball. It was really disappointing but I remember the City fans still singing for us at the end.

Spurs went on to beat Chelsea in the final that year and we settled for staying in Division Two. Looking back, it will always be the game I remember for many different reasons. I survived it even though Cyril Knowles did his best to make sure I didn't and we had a decent side which competed with one of the best teams I had played against. So, although we were beaten, it gave us a bit of hope to see we could give the big sides a real game and, more importantly, in that cup run we had given the fans something to shout about.

Our manager Fred Ford left in 1967 and chairman Harry Dolman brought in Alan Dicks who had been assistant to Jimmy Hill at Coventry City. I don't think Dicksy rated me really and the writing was on the wall when I went out on loan for a few games to Mansfield Town. I wasn't really interested in a move there but at least I was playing. When I returned to City it was clear

I wasn't in the manager's plans so my contract more or less ran out and I was made redundant.

Then completely out of the blue I got a call from Paris Saint-Germain in France asking whether I would be interested in coming to them. Now you have to remember they were not the Paris Saint-Germain of today – they had just won the second division in France and were on their way up. They had contact with Arsenal and had asked the Gunners if there were any players they could recommend. Arsenal recommended me as they had tried to sign me as a kid and I think they just followed my progress throughout my career which was really flattering. I really did have a lot to think about. There were family things to consider, it was a foreign country and I knew nothing really about the club or the type of football they played. But after all that, I remember thinking, this could be a real adventure, plus I'm nearly 30 and this might just be the experience I need. I signed and became one of the first foreign players to play in France.

I lived on the outskirts of Paris on my own for six months before Patsy and the family joined me. The game was really different from the British game and I think it really suited me. It was all about skill and technique which really was my game; I was encouraged to run at defenders. I enjoyed it but homesickness really kicked in for all the family and I left after a season returning to our home in Bristol. I had to make some decisions as there were a few clubs after my services but I was not getting any younger and, like many players of that era, I had to think about what I was going to do when my career was finished so I could provide for my family.

As luck would have it I was also approached to work as a financial rep for a large bank. I took the job as it was a no-brainer for me. I didn't hang up the boots entirely as I played part-time for Bath City and various local sides around the area. I am so glad to have been asked to take part in this book as I know I was a bit like marmite for the supporters: some liked me and some thought I didn't do enough in games. One thing I think we all agree on is that we all love this club and I will look back and think how privileged I was to pull on that red shirt.

DARIUSZ DZIEKANOWSKI

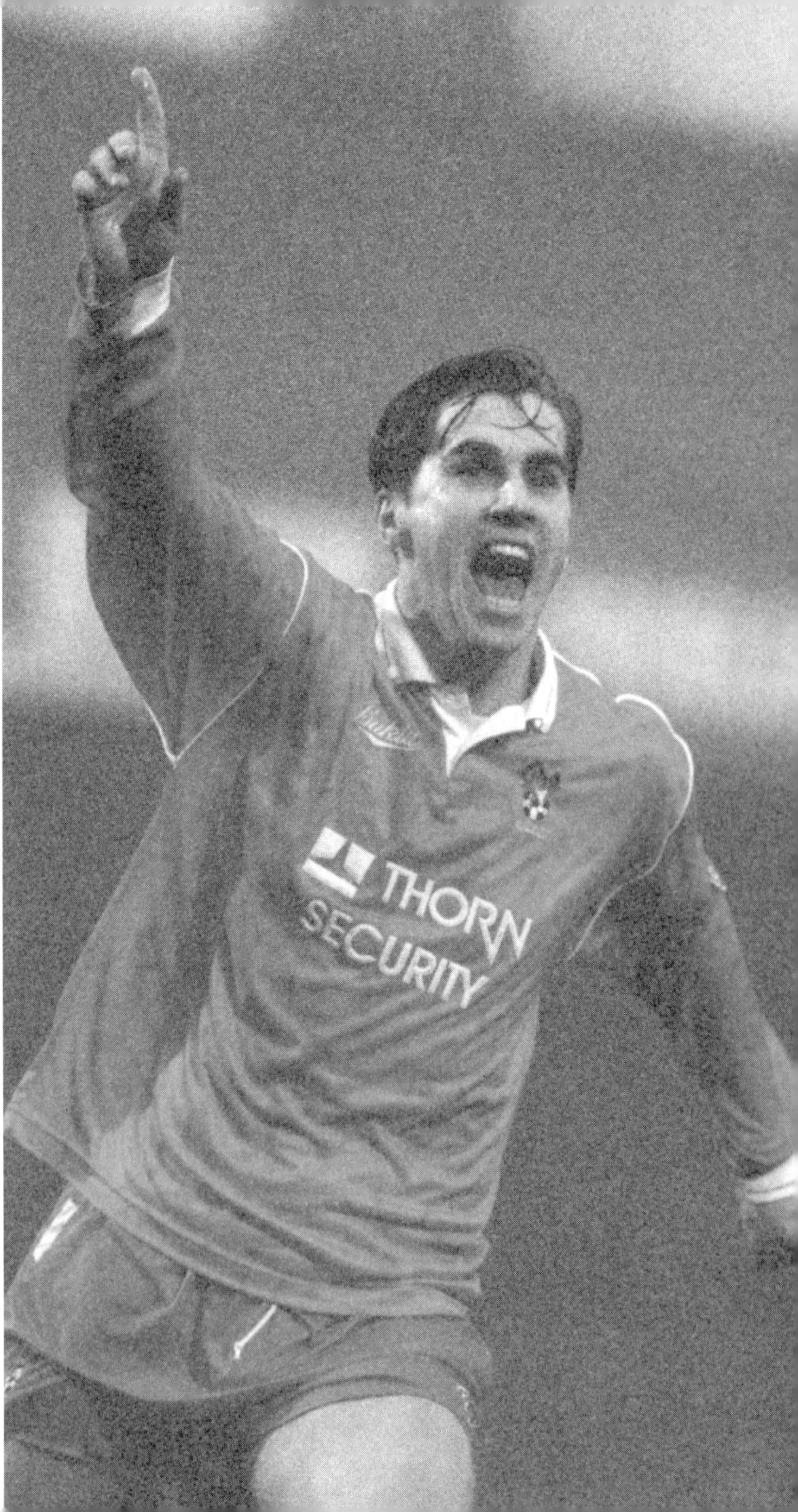

Dariusz 'Jacki' Dziekanowski

As the iron curtain opened across eastern Europe in the early nineties, a player the like of which Bristol City had never seen arrived at Ashton Gate via Scottish giants Glasgow Celtic. Dariusz 'Jacki' Dziekanowski was a Polish international who oozed class and pedigree. He made his name at Celtic Park and the fans in green and white were in shock when he was sold to Bristol City for £225,000 in the 1991/92 season. Jacki hit the ground running, lighting up Bristol City under the management of Jimmy Lumsden and then later Denis Smith. And it was under Smith that he truly flourished, forging an unbeatable partnership with striker Andy Cole. Jacki was without doubt a true maverick, inconsistent at times, but when he was on song the Ashton Gate faithful loved everything about him. Unfortunately as Smith was sacked and Andy Cole was sold for big money, the Pole found himself out of favour with new player-manager Russell Osman and in favour with some of Bristol's nightspots. Jacki eventually left the club within 18 months of joining, citing homesickness and a need for a fresh challenge. Such was the fans' displeasure over the exit that they booed Osman after he scored for City on the day Jacki left. Over the years his exploits on and off the field have given him true legend status amongst City fans of a certain age. One thing is for sure, he was one of the most talented players ever to grace Ashton Gate.

Bristol City 2 Wolverhampton Wanderers 0
Football League Second Division
17 March 1992
Ashton Gate

Bristol City: Welch, Llewellyn, Scott, Aizlewood, Bryant, Osman, Mellon, Edwards, Cole, Allison, May. Sub: Dziekanowski.

Goals: Dziekanowski 2.

It is such an honour to be asked to contribute to this wonderful book *Match of my Life*. I am deeply touched that the supporters of Bristol City remember me, although I will always be grateful to them for taking me into their hearts. I was very upset when I left the club all those years ago, so it's great for me to tell them now how much they all meant to me.

My journey to Bristol started in Warsaw, Poland. I was born there and I was, according to my parents, obsessed with football from the moment I could walk. My grandfather always used to tell me that I would stop and watch a game even when I was a toddler. My grandparents owned a four-storey house in Warsaw and apparently I used to climb to the very top of it and look out of the window, as from that vantage point, you could see a football pitch with people playing on it and I was transfixed by the game. I joined my local side Polonia Warsaw at 11 and stayed with them until I was 17 when I and a lot of other young prospects were signed by the major local team Gwardia Warszawa.

My career in Poland went well and I made my international debut in a 0–0 draw against France in Paris. I think I was around 20 years old at the time. My career really took off when I signed for Legia Warsaw. I won the Polish Cup and I was now a regular for the national side. I was there for about four years but unfortunately a new coach arrived during my last year and we didn't really see eye to eye on some things, mainly me and my contribution to the side. It was interesting times across

Europe then with the start of the Berlin Wall coming down and there were opportunities for eastern European sportsmen, especially footballers. Agents had appeared and they were a new thing in the game, as before you just got told by the club what you would get and for how long you would get it. It was similar to football in the United Kingdom back in the 1950s.

Anyway, an agent contacted me and told me he could get me a move abroad which I really fancied. I had a couple of offers but the one that stuck out for me was Glasgow Celtic. I had played against them in Europe and I remember their fans were crazy in the home leg; they made a lot of noise in the away leg too. I met Celtic manager Billy McNeill and I signed for them. At the time they were in the shadow of neighbours Rangers who were dominating the league under manager Graeme Souness. I enjoyed my time in Scotland and the fans really took to me; we had a good side with players like Paul McStay, Paul Elliott, Chris Morris and Packie Bonner. But it was very difficult to break the Rangers hold on the title. I scored in some memorable games up there, a couple against Rangers, which always helped with getting the fans on your side. And, of course, the one game from my time in Scotland was the European Cup Winners' Cup tie against Partizan Belgrade where I scored four goals in the second leg at Celtic Park after we were losing 2–1 from the first leg. It was a magical night as we won 5–4 but unfortunately went out on away goals.

In 1991 Billy McNeill was sacked and I was very upset. I liked Billy a lot; he had won the European Cup with Celtic and was a real legend. I enjoyed listening to his stories from those days and he really looked after me while I was there. He was replaced by former Arsenal player and youth coach Liam Brady. It was plain from the start that I was not Brady's type of player. He didn't think I worked hard enough and that may have been true but I gave everything on the pitch and all I wanted was the ball. I eventually left about ten months after his appointment, the nail in the coffin being when he signed Tony Cascarino as my replacement whilst I was still there. Offers came in and I was just happy to play football, so I didn't really care where I went as long as it was a good standard of football. Some teams were obviously put off as I had gained a bit of a reputation as a luxury player they might not need. The best offer was from Bristol City.

I met manager Jimmy Lumsden who had played for Celtic back in the day. He spoke to me and told me they had been watching me for a while and I might be just what they needed to boost the team who were in the middle of Division Two, which is now the Championship. I had a further meeting with Jimmy and the Bristol City chairman and I remember I could not understand the chairman's English but I could understand Jimmy's Scottish, so Jimmy had to translate for me. We got there in the end and I signed in 1992 for £225,000. I had no clue about Bristol but I did know it had a bridge, called the Clifton Suspension Bridge which I remembered from one of my schoolbooks.

The team I joined were in a bit of a rut. They had just lost manager Joe Jordan and Jimmy had taken over which to be fair had lifted spirits. They had some good players at the club, particularly a young lad called Junior Bent who was the quickest player I had ever seen. I made my debut at home against Southend United and got a tremendous reception from the fans although I missed an absolute golden chance in the first minute, but they stuck with me and I rewarded them and Jimmy later in the second half when I scored. We drew the game 2–2 and I really felt at home. Another game I remember was an FA Cup tie away at Leicester City. I was thrilled to play in the FA Cup as I had seen finals back home in Poland when I was a little boy. The highlights of the game were shown that night on the *Match of the Day* programme and many supporters I speak to today mention the game. We won the match 2–1 with myself and Junior Bent getting the goals and I really did run the midfield that day; it was one of my great games for the club.

The one that I will always remember is a league game against Wolverhampton Wanderers. Jimmy had left the club and the new manager was Denis Smith. I liked Denis. He told me he was going to build a side around me and a young lad he was initially going to get on loan with an option to buy from Arsenal, Andy Cole. Anyway, we played Wolves away in the March and

Denis was struggling with results – I think we had not won for 11 games so the pressure was on him and us. We drew the game 1–1 but after 15 minutes the Wolves player Derek Mountfield – yes, I still remember his name – came crashing through me and split my shin pad along with my shin. I lay there screaming in Polish and I was carried off to the dressing room. Blood was pouring from the gash on my leg and City had their doctor there who looked at it and told me I needed 15 stitches. He said he would do them now. I couldn't believe it – I told him at Celtic I would be taken to hospital and he gently reminded me that I was no longer at Celtic so he stitched me up.

I missed the following games against Plymouth Argyle and Cambridge United, both of which we lost, and by a quirk of fate the next game was Wolves at home some ten days after we first met them. Denis told me he needed me and said I would be on the bench and hopefully come on late. I had not trained all week and the doctor was not happy as he explained to Dennis and myself that if so much as a ball struck the stitches they could open up again. Denis looked at me and reiterated that I was needed so I became sub. It was a real night of tension at Ashton Gate. There was a full house and it was under floodlights. The atmosphere reminded me of the night at Celtic Park when I got the four goals – it was electric. The supporters were with Denis and the lads but I think a bad display or a defeat could well have cost him his job that night. It was really frustrating on the bench; I really wanted to come on but I was also worried that I might not do myself justice and could injure the shin and be out for longer. Wolves' big danger man was Steve Bull but our two centre-backs Mark Aizlewood and Russell Osman kept him quiet in the first half and we had a few chances up front with young Andy Cole who had just joined and Wayne Allison. I really liked Andy; you could see he was going to be a top footballer. I had seen him train with us whilst I was on the sidelines and I knew we could have a great partnership when I got fit.

The first half ended 0–0 and the fans clapped us off as we had given a very good account of ourselves but without any finish. Denis spoke to me at half-time and told me if it stayed like this he was going to bring me on. We went out in the second half and again it was very close. The game became more and more tense as it went on, and with about 20 minutes to go, Denis told me to get warmed up. As I stepped out from the dugout the Williams Stand behind me cheered and clapped. I suddenly forgot about the shin and I couldn't wait to get on. Denis threw me on in place of Rob Edwards and it was a tactical switch. He told me to sit behind the two strikers Cole and Allison and get the ball behind the Wolves back four so Andy could run on to it. The move in style worked almost right away as I picked up the ball in midfield and thread a pass through to Andy and he hit the post. The fans got louder and louder and the minutes ticked by. I noticed my old mate Derek Mountfield coming looking for me but I just rode a few of his challenges and Wayne Allison, our big centre-forward, gave him a few whacks every time he came near me.

We had about six minutes left when a ball was played up to Wayne and he flicked it on to me so I just hit it goalwards and it flew in. The crowd and the players went wild as I did. I ran to the bench and Denis Smith punched the air towards the Williams Stand. I was eventually caught by my team-mates and they just hugged me and kissed me. The crowd never had chance to draw breath before I played a lovely one-two with Andy Cole and I found myself bearing down on the Wolves goal, so I stuck it past their keeper. The noise the fans made was incredible. You would have thought we had won the European Cup; supporters were on the pitch, the stands were all on their feet and people were jumping all over each other. By the time the cheering had stopped the ref blew for full time and we went off to a heroes' applause.

The Wolves team looked shell-shocked over what had happened to them. As I came off Denis grabbed me and thanked me. Looking back, it was a bigger night for me than the Cup Winners' Cup tie at Celtic Park against Partizan Belgrade. Although I had got four goals in that, this was special as I was injured and had only been given 20 minutes of football to play. I was also thrilled for Denis and the fans as they had been through a rough time. Yes, the game will stay with me forever; it was a fantastic night to be involved in.

As the season progressed my partnership with Andy Cole flourished and we played really well together, often being featured on national TV, which was great for the club. Things started to pick up but then we hit some terrible form and after a 2–0 defeat to Luton Town in the FA Cup Denis was sacked. The new man was centre-half Russell Osmond. I know it must have been difficult for Russell making the move from player to manager and he did well but I was certainly not in his plans. The club also sold Andy Cole to Newcastle United for £1.75m. The move worked out well for Andy as he certainly fulfilled his potential as a striker, going on after Newcastle United to play for Manchester United and England.

For me, I was in and out of the side and it was clear that Osman did not look at me as his type of player, which is football I suppose. I became disillusioned with things and as I was young and single I started to enjoy the nightlife of Bristol a bit too much. Osman always knew when I had been out, and the trouble was I would turn up for training but I knew I wouldn't be playing Saturday so I think I fell out of love with the club and football in general. I have to say, though, some of the stories about my time in the nightclubs of Bristol are very funny and not exactly 100 per cent true but it gives the supporters a laugh and certainly plays into this image I had as a playboy in Bristol at that time. My relationship with the manager really was at rock bottom at that time and in the end I left the club in 1993. I really was heartbroken to go and I was gutted I never got to say goodbye to the fans but in football you rarely do when it comes to a transfer.

I went back to Legia Warsaw and my career just drifted from there really. I had spells in Switzerland and Germany before finishing back in Poland with Polonia Warsaw where it had all begun for me. Those years after leaving City were not great. I would have loved to have stayed in English or Scottish football but I think I had this reputation of not being a team player, which I really dispute, and the fallout from that was that clubs thought I would be trouble if they signed me.

When I am asked where I played my best football I have to say it was those 18 months with Denis Smith at Bristol City. I played over 60 games for Poland and appeared in World Cups but those games in the red shirt of City will be my best memories. I remember being asked to go back to Ashton Gate for Andy Llewellyn's testimonial and I was really nervous, as I didn't know what sort of reception I would get. When they sang my name I filled up with tears; it was wonderful, as was meeting up with Andy Cole again who turned up to play in the game.

Today I have a successful media career with TV and newspapers in Poland. I am also the UEFA delegate for Poland and I have in the past been number two with the national side which was a real honour. I never really saw my future in coaching as I like my family to be settled and with coaching you have to go where the jobs are. I have been back to Bristol City many times as a guest of the club and the facilities at the stadium are incredible. They certainly are a Premier League club off the pitch. Their results are the first I look for at home in Poland and my dream is that they will be in the Premier League soon. When I look back on my time at the club I am humbled by the high esteem that supporters hold me in considering I was only there 18 months. I really think the club could have gone on and done something good with the side we had but it was not to be. At least I have my memories, especially that great night against Wolves where everything seemed to fit into place.

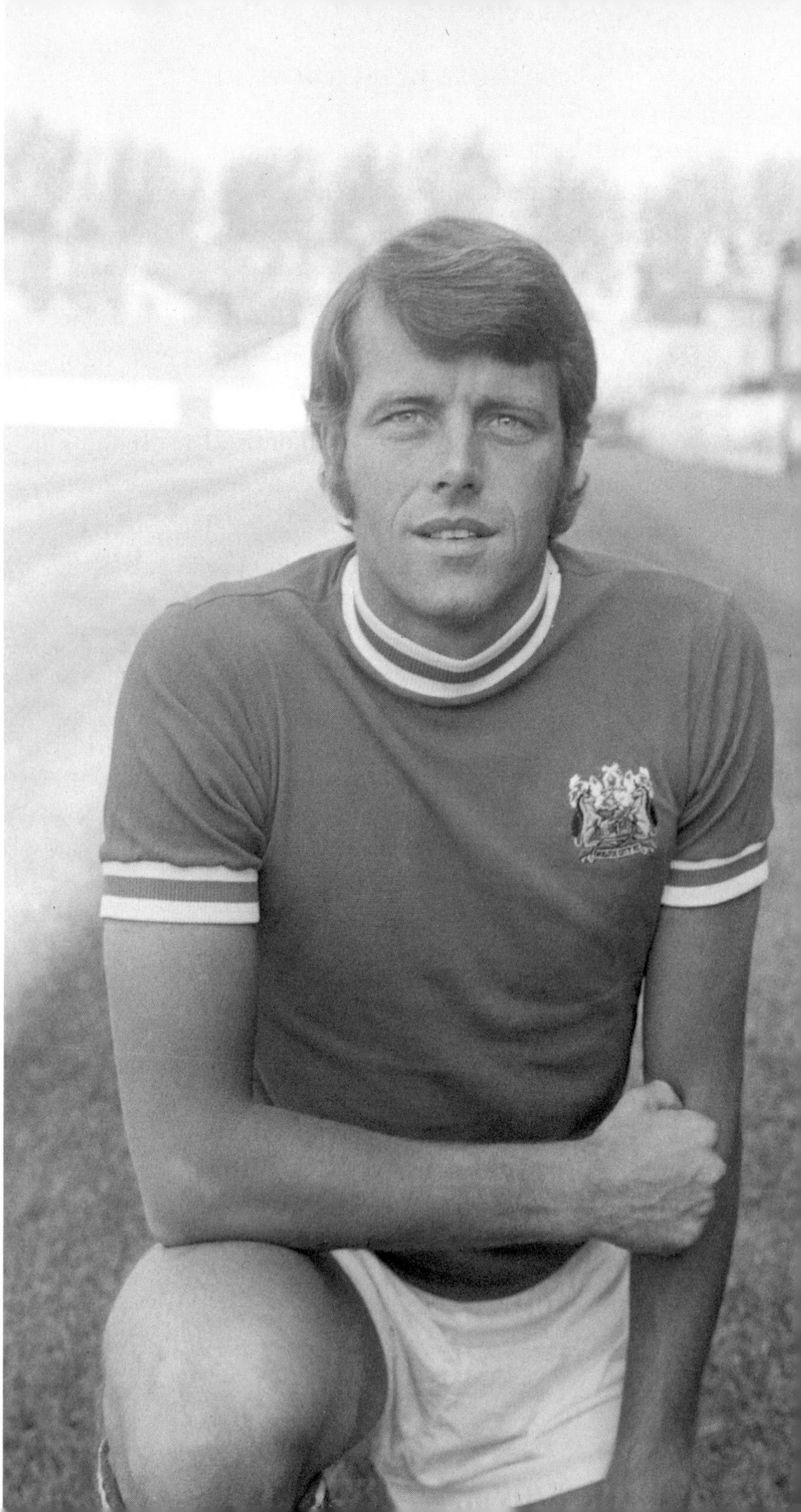

JOHN GALLEY

John Galley

When it comes to making a first impression at a new club nobody could hold a candle to Bristol City striker John Galley. A product of the famous Wolverhampton Wanderers youth setup, this brave, strong forward scored on his debut for Wolves, got hat-tricks on his Rotherham United and Bristol City debuts, along with goals in his first games for Nottingham Forest, Peterborough and Hereford United. And what makes his hat-trick for Bristol City the stuff of legends is that he arrived at the club on crutches due to a foot injury.

During his stay at Ashton Gate his contribution to the club was immense. Twice in the late sixties his goals kept the club from relegation to the Third Division and almost certainly kept manager Alan Dicks in a job. A real fans' favourite, he led the City forward line with bravery, good touch with either foot and a heading ability so strong that it was like a full-blown shot. His unselfish approach to the game earned the respect of all those around him. Surprisingly in 1972 the club accepted a £33,000 offer from Nottingham Forest and John returned to the Midlands. At Forest he never emulated the success at City and after a successful loan period at Peterborough, he came back to the West Country to join former City number two John Sillett who was managing Hereford United. Galley will always be held in great esteem by City fans of a certain age who will fondly remember 'Gall-eey, Gall-eey' ringing around the ground.

Huddersfield Town 0 Bristol City 3
Football League Second Division
16 December 1967
Leeds Road

Bristol City: Gibson, Parr, Briggs, Wimshurst, Connor, Bush, Crowe, Garland, Galley, Quigley, Bartley.

Goals: Galley 3.

Wow, what a fantastic opportunity for me to talk about the 'Match of my Life'. Over the years I have certainly had many to choose from, mostly all debuts due to the fact that I scored in all of them; they will always be the games that I remember most fondly. And Bristol City go hand in hand with that as I had such a great time at the club.

My introduction to football was when I signed for Wolverhampton Wanderers as a 16-year-old. I had given up an apprenticeship as a bricklayer to sign but play football was all I wanted to do. The club were managed by the legendary Stan Cullis and he took a real interest in the youngsters, particularly as we had just been beaten 2–1 in the FA Youth Cup by Newcastle United. Stan was very proud of us and really encouraged us to take the next step and get into the first team. I got my chance away at Fulham. I must have been about 17 years of age and the club was littered with great players like Peter Broadbent, Ron Flowers and Bobby Woodruff. I managed to score at Craven Cottage in a 5–0 demolition of Fulham but my chances in the side were very limited due to the professionals at the club who were in front of me. In total I think I played five games for the Wolves and scored two goals, but when Rotherham came in for me I knew I would be playing every week. So although the move was gut-wrenching, as Wolves was all I knew and I had just met my wife Elizabeth there, it was something I had to do for myself and my career. I signed for Rotherham and really hit the ground running, getting a hat-trick on my debut against Coventry City. I enjoyed my time at the club and, as predicted, I was playing regularly. I became good friends with former Bristol City player Bobby Williams who provided lots of goals for me at the time. I remember Bob singing the praises of Bristol City then, and saying if you get the chance go; they will love you there.

Well I'm sure Bob said something to the powers that be at Ashton Gate because weeks later I got asked into the manager's office and was told Bristol City had made a bid for me. Bob always tells me he got me the move which I always laugh at. Trouble was, City manager Alan Dicks wanted to meet me but at the time I was recovering from a foot injury and was in plaster. Alan was fine about it and I came down on the train to meet him. He told me later that the directors were very unhappy that they had signed somebody in plaster but Alan told them it would be worth it. I was due to have the plaster off the next week and would be fit to play the following week. Anyway, the game was postponed due to snow so I had more time for the foot to recover for the away game at Huddersfield Town. As I was still living in Yorkshire I drove to Leeds Road in the morning and had not even met my City team-mates until I walked in the dressing room. And so this leads me to the 'Match of my Life'.

It was unbelievable really, but I have to say what a start for me at Bristol City. I felt at home right away. There were some big characters in the dressing room and considering the side were struggling we had a good team, with Mike Gibson in goal, who was a fantastic keeper and would be so brave, and Ken Wimshurst at the back, who had arrived just before me from Southampton. Ken was immaculate both on and off the field. He was like a Rolls-Royce. He never got flustered and would always look for that pass, he inspired confidence and read the game brilliantly. His partner was Jack Connor who was the joker in the changing rooms and one of the bravest centre-halves I ever saw – he would stick his head in anywhere. And we also had Johnny Quigley who drove the team on – he was never-ending with his tackling and was a great foil for me with his link-up play around the box.

I had a few nerves before the match but that was understandable as I wanted to do well for myself and also Alan Dicks who had a bit of grief from the directors about signing me. I have to say we were all pumped up for it. Manager Dicks had a game plan and that was for Johnny Quigley to follow Huddersfield's Nicholson all over the park, as Nicholson was the best attacking wing-half in the division and Alan knew he would cause us problems if we gave him too much room. We matched them man for man in the first couple of minutes and it felt like I had been playing with them for years. You have to bear in mind I had not even trained with City up till that point. We were on top and put together a lovely move starting from keeper Mike Gibson and involving the back four, midfield and eventually myself, but just as I was about to stick it in the net the ball bobbled and I stuck it almost out of the ground. I certainly did not want to look up at the directors' box where Alan Dicks was sat with a few of the City directors. The lads just got on with it but I was determined to get another chance and on about 30 minutes a ball was played into the Huddersfield box by Chris Crowe, it was headed back out of the box and just sat nicely for me to volley it into the net with the keeper helpless. The goal silenced the home fans and the lads just jumped all over me. We went in at half-time 1–0 up and Alan Dicks had come down from the directors' box early to greet us as we came in. He was overjoyed with the goal and was equally pleased with Johnny Quigley's performance who had made sure Nicholson had not had a kick all first half. Jack Connor and Alec Briggs had also had fantastic first halves in defence, making sure nothing got through. I spent half-time chatting to young Chris Garland who was one of the promising youngsters at the club. He was all ears as I told him that I would continue to hold the ball up and flick it on for him to run on to as I really didn't see anybody in the Huddersfield back four to stop us.

We went out for the second half fired right up and Chris got on the end of one or two of my flicks and very nearly got on the scoresheet himself. Then on 70 minutes a ball played from Chris Crowe was flicked on by myself and Chris went after it. He hustled the defender and I went after them both. Eventually the ball broke loose to me on the edge of the box and I steered it into the corner of the net with my left foot. When I think back now, we really were on fire that afternoon, and I don't think any team in the country could have stopped us. I remember thinking, I'm going to love it here. Ten minutes later a high clearance from Ken Wimshurst sent the ball upfield. I was in my own half but I raced after it with two Huddersfield defenders in tow. As the keeper ran out to get the ball we arrived at the same time and the ball cannoned off him on to me and flew into the net. I couldn't believe it as the lads picked me up from the mud to celebrate. I remember running back to the centre circle and seeing manager Alan Dicks on his feet applauding in the directors' box. It was a feeling that I have always remembered to this day. I also remember just before the final whistle I had a header from a Garland cross that was cleared off the line, but I was more than happy with the hat-trick. I remember the dressing room at the end was manic. Alan Dicks gave me a massive bear hug telling me how pleased he was. I also remember one of the directors telling me it was the first hat-trick a City player had scored since John Atyeo's against Shrewsbury in 1965. I sat on the dressing room bench and just had a quiet five minutes thinking about what had just happened and I knew this was the club for me.

All the directors came over and shook my hand. That was quite funny, especially regarding what they had said when I signed. I said goodbye to the lads and drove home not realising I had not even got the ball.

After a few weeks I moved down to Bristol with my family and really felt part of the club. That season I ended up with 18 goals in 21 matches which meant I was the club's top scorer. I remember a vital away win at Charlton where myself and Chris Crowe scored and that result really gave us the belief that we could stay up. It was great to play alongside Chris as I had been with him at Wolves and we really played well together. In the end the goals kept us up as we finished fourth from bottom, narrowly escaping relegation. Although we struggled that season we had some good players, particularly young Chris Garland who partnered me up front. Chris was a class act on and off the field and he was always willing to learn from an older player. I was really pleased when he got his big move to Chelsea years later.

My career at City went from strength to strength and I was near enough always the club's leading scorer, which I always thought of as an indication that I was doing my job. I used to be filled with pride when the old East End used to sing 'Gall-eey, Gall-eey'. In total I had played 172 games for the Robins and scored 84 goals, which was not a bad return. But then I got the call to go to Alan Dicks's office as it looked like a move was on the cards. Alan explained to me that there had been a bid from Nottingham Forest who had just been relegated from Division One and they were looking to get straight back. Manager Dave Mackay had singled me out as the man to get the goals to do it. Forest had offered £30,000 which was decent money and the

City board had accepted it, so I went to speak to Dave Mackay. As I was walking through the Ashton Gate reception I saw Bobby Gould coming towards me. I had known Bobby since his Wolves days and he said, 'Hello, John. What you up too?' I told him that I was going to Nottingham to possibly sign for Forest. He looked shocked and said, 'Well, I'm coming here to hopefully play alongside you.' We laughed and off I went and signed for Forest. Looking back, I'm not sure what the club had told Bobby but he did sign and have a good career at Ashton Gate in the end.

For me, the City Ground, Nottingham, wasn't the career success I had hoped for. I started off with a goal on my debut against Fulham but, weeks after signing, Dave Mackay left to take over at rivals Derby County and Allan Brown came in as manager. My chances in the side became limited and, although I had scored a few, I really had no run in the team. It was clear that Brown did not rate me and that's fine as football is all about opinions but the difference with Brown was that a lot of it was personal. He never really spoke and when I went to see him he refused to let me go or even put me on loan. This became really difficult and although I was back in the Midlands I felt as though my career was stalling after the good times at Ashton Gate. I was sold the idea that Forest were going to give Division Two a real go but I got the feeling that a lot of the players thought they were too good for Division Two and didn't really put a shift in in games.

In the end, after various clubs showed an interest in me, Peterborough, who were managed by Noel Cantwell, asked if they could take me on loan. Surprisingly Brown said yes and I suddenly found myself at training with a smile on my face. Unfortunately the loan period was only for seven games and in that time I managed to get on the scoresheet on my debut. Noel Cantwell asked Forest if they would consider selling me but Brown refused. I was bitterly disappointed and found myself knocking about in Forest's reserves.

Then my two-year nightmare ended at Forest with an offer from Hereford United who were managed by John Sillett, who had been assistant to Alan Dicks at City. I nearly ripped Hereford's hands off when I got the offer. I signed and spent three good seasons at the club, even winning the Third Division championship in 1976. After that I played non-league for Telford before hanging up my boots.

Today I'm retired and still go to the odd Nottingham Forest game as it's my local team. I also get down to Ashton Gate for different functions and I love the response I get from the fans who still remember me. Some even shout 'Gall-eey, Gall-eey' when they see me. My time at City is very precious to me. I always think it was the place I played some of my best football and I really grew as a player. The club will always be dear to me and that's why, even after all my debut goals, the City debut will always be the 'Match of my Life'.

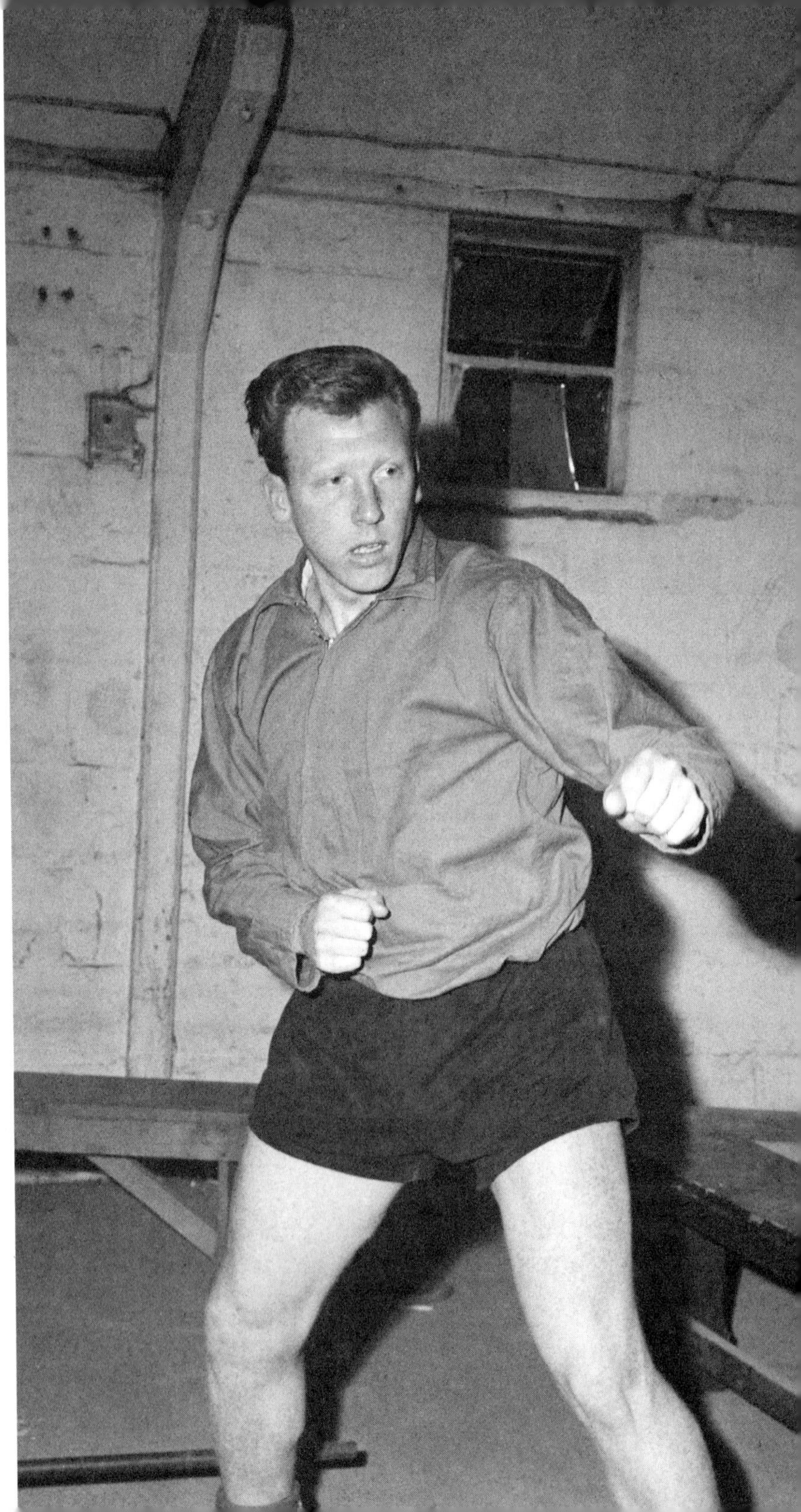

MIKE GIBSON

Mike Gibson

When Bristol City manager Fred Ford paid Shrewsbury Town £5,000 for goalkeeper Mike Gibson, Ford knew the fee was pretty steep in terms of the Robins' usual purchases. But after watching the young Gibson in various matches for the Shrews he knew he had got it right.

Mike Gibson is a City man through and through, a keeper who by today's criteria would never have got an opportunity to make a living as a goalkeeper due to his 5ft 9in stance. But for Mike, what he lacked in height he more than made up for in bravery and timing. The Derby-born youngster arrived from Shrewsbury to replace fans' favourite Tony Cook in the 1962/63 season. Gibson became an instant hit with the Ashton Gate faithful, particularly the old East End part of the ground, which was situated behind the goal. They cheered his every move, especially his warm-up which consisted of striding four paces from the goal line, marking a line with his boot then four steps back and finishing with a jump to touch the crossbar. Gibson's skill in front of goal saw him a stalwart of the 1964/65 team that gained promotion to Division Two. In 1972, after ten years' service with the Robins, Mike was sold to Gillingham to make way for emerging City youngster Ray Cashley. He had made 376 appearances for the club during that time. But his love affair with the Robins did not end there as he was brought back to the club in the 1980s by manager Terry Cooper, where he filled a number of roles from scout to reserve-team boss. He truly has Bristol City running through his veins and he will always be thought of as City's greatest keeper.

Tottenham Hotspur 2 Bristol City 0 (AET)
League Cup semi-final second leg
23 December 1970
White Hart Lane

Bristol City: Gibson, Jacobs, Drysdale, Wimshurst, Rooks, Parr, Skirton, Garland, Sharpe, Gow, Spiring. Sub: Tainton.

I was born in Derby and I always wanted to be a footballer and for some strange reason a goalkeeper at that. I was playing for my county at that time and I remember the thrill and excitement throughout my whole family when I got the letter to say I had been picked for England Schoolboys. I played against Switzerland at Brighton's Goldstone Ground in 1956 where we drew 2–2. I only played that one game and I remember being disappointed that it was not at Wembley and also thinking, well, maybe that is as far as I will go in the game, as playing for England Schoolboys was the pinnacle for a lot of lads who never made the grade.

I was watched by numerous clubs but remember West Bromwich Albion being interested, but nothing happened. I gained an apprenticeship on the railways and my dad was very keen for me to finish that as I don't think he thought there was a living to be made in football, and to be honest there was certainly more money on the railways. I started playing part-time football for Gresty Rovers and I was invited up to Blackpool for a week to play in a practice game. The game was incredible. I don't remember the score but I do remember the opposition side was Blackpool and it was full of first-teamers like Stanley Matthews and Stan Mortensen. To say I was star-struck was an understatement. I was homesick that week and never really had any thoughts of signing for them as I still had a year to go on my apprenticeship which ended the following year.

I was happy playing part-time football with Burton Albion and a couple of other local clubs before I got my chance at Shrewsbury Town. I enjoyed my time there. We had a decent side and got to the League Cup semi-finals in 1961, losing 4–3 over two legs to Rotherham. The tournament was in its infancy back then and there was no Wembley appearance for the finalists, just a home and away two-legged final. I remember being aware of the interest of Bristol City; Shrewsbury always let me know when there was somebody in the stand from City watching me and it was usually Robins manager Fred Ford. I remember one game against Peterborough where I literally had a storming game for the Shrews and I was told later that it was that game that got me the move to the south-west. It was a real change of life for me when I signed as I had just got married and here I was moving down south to a bigger club.

I knew very little about City when I signed other than they were in the Third Division like Shrewsbury but, as I said, a much bigger club in every sense.

I have so many great memories of matches I have played in for Bristol City. My debut against Crystal Palace was fantastic. The City fans gave me a great reception and, although the game ended 1–1, I thought I had a good game. The local press did, too, which always helps you settle in. I remember that first season meeting a lot of the fans after games home and away, and it was during this interaction with them that they all told me how much they loved my prematch ritual of marking a line four paces from the goal line then touching the crossbar. I told them the line was so I would not lose my bearings in terms of positioning during the game. They would all cheer as I did it and also count the four paces there and back. It gave me such a fantastic feeling before the game. It felt like the whole of the East End terrace was helping me keep the ball out and also helped me settle in in my first season. I also remember a game against Wolverhampton Wanderers at Molineux where I must have kept every shot out. The local press said I had 'defied the laws of gravity and possibility in keeping Wolves out'. I don't know about that description but I certainly asked our defence in the dressing room after the game where they were during the 90 minutes.

Another game I remember was in the 1964/65 season where we clinched promotion to Division Two against Oldham at Ashton Gate. The atmosphere that day was incredible. We had the great John Atyeo up front and one of the best sides I had ever played in, with the likes of Gordon Parr, Brian Clark and Alec Briggs. I remember many thought we would never get the chance of promotion, especially my good friend Peter Godsiff who wrote for the *Bristol Evening Post* and travelled on the coach with us. Peter wrote after a defeat against Mansfield that we had blown any chance of promotion, and I'm sure Pete must have done it to gee us up because after the article came out we went on something like a ten-match unbeaten run, which culminated in that game against Oldham Athletic.

The fans that day were incredible. They were willing us to get the win for the club but also for Big John who was such an icon for the fans and was coming to the end of his career. The game was really tense with around 30,000 packed into Ashton Gate. If I remember rightly, Mansfield, who were chasing us in the league, were away at Barnsley and they had to score three goals for every one City scored. All of a sudden word got round the ground that Mansfield were 2–0 up in the opening 20 minutes. Things calmed down just before half-time when Brian Clark scored for us. I was really busy second half but the defence was brilliant, and with minutes to go the fairy tale happened and John smashed a ball into the Oldham top corner sending the place wild. That was it. We had won 2–0 and Mansfield had won 3–2 so unbelievably we were promoted by 0.11 of a goal, if that makes any sense. It was a very special memory. People were crying at the end of the game, Big John included, and I remember going to the Towns Talk club just outside Bristol, which was a bit of a regular for some of the players. I think I drank myself sober with champagne. Chairman Harry Dolman gave a speech and promised manager Fred Ford a job for life, so you can tell how drunk he was. As I said, we had a really good side and almost went up the following year into Division One but were pipped by Southampton in the end.

The game I am choosing, though, is one that was towards the end of my time at Bristol City and strangely enough a match where we did not win, but for various reasons it will always stay with me. It was a game where I came so close to realising one of my ambitions and that was to play at Wembley. It was also a game in which I felt so much disappointment and realised that, although the critics hailed me as the man of the match, as a defeat it took ages to get over, not only for me but the team.

We were languishing around the bottom half of Division Two when we went on our League Cup run. We had beaten Rotherham, Blackpool, Leicester City and Fulham before finding ourselves with a two-legged semi-final against the mighty Spurs. We never thought about getting to Wembley until we beat Leicester City in round four. I don't know what it was but we all started to think maybe we could do this. The Spurs team were packed with stars: they had Pat Jennings, Alan Mullery, Alan Gilzean, not to mention Martin Peters and Martin Chivers up front. Our manager Alan Dicks instilled belief in us and we just wanted to go to the second game still in the match.

The first leg at Ashton Gate drew a crowd of 30,000 and although Spurs were a top side we matched them man for man and went in at half-time with all things equal at 0–0. The second half saw us go 1–0 up through Alan Skirton, and Ashton Gate erupted. Spurs piled on the pressure and late on Alan Gilzean equalised with a header that I just couldn't stop. It was mixed emotions coming off as we were happy to still be in the tie but gutted to have let the goal in. The press were extremely complimentary of us and everything was building to the second leg at White Hart Lane on the following Wednesday. Manager Alan Dicks made a massive call before the second leg by dropping centre-forward John Galley after John had struggled in the last few games. He replaced John with young 20-year-old local lad Peter Spiring, who had only featured for us on and off.

We drove up to London for the second leg the night before and stayed in a hotel. Everyone was in good spirits and we really thought we had a chance. It had been a very long time since Bristol City were anywhere near getting to a Wembley final and here we were just 90 minutes away from achieving it, although we knew what a massive task stood in front of us as Spurs were in the top six of Division One at the time. Yet we had matched them once and we could do it again. Going to the ground was incredible; we couldn't believe how many City fans had made the trip, especially on a wet Wednesday night. But made it they had and they never stopped singing inside and outside the ground. The stadium even then was way beyond what we were used to in Division Two. There were individual baths and you had your own sitting area and hangers for your clothes, as opposed to a peg that we were used to. Alan Dicks gathered us round and gave us a team talk, pointing out things we could improve on and how they might play. Then the bell sounded and out we ran into the packed, floodlit White Hart Lane. I did my usual ritual and could hear the City fans away at one corner of the ground cheering as I jumped and touched the crossbar.

The game started as you would imagine, a really tense affair with both sides not giving much away. I pushed a Gilzean header over the bar and dived to retrieve the ball from Martin Chivers after the subsequent corner. We went in at half-time 0–0 and our confidence was sky-high. Alan Dicks told us to keep it going and I remember giving Ken Wimshurst, our centre-half, a few words regarding marking Alan Gilzean.

The second half sprung into life with chances for both teams but as the night went on I had a sense that maybe extra time or penalties were looming to settle this one. Spurs threw everything at us and I remember diving numerous times at the feet of Martin Peters and Martin Chivers to win the ball. Then the ref blew and it was extra time. Alan Dicks got us into a huddle and explained how we had come through three replays to get here and we had held a team like Spurs with all their stars over two matches. I looked around the side and we were absolutely knackered; you could see it on our faces.

Then in extra time I made a real error of judgement. A free kick from Cyril Knowles went high into the air and I advanced too soon. By the time I had realised my mistake and checked back, Martin Chivers rose high in the air and crashed a header home. I literally felt sick. Unfortunately ten minutes later Jimmy Pearce crashed a volley into the net from outside the box. We had a couple of chances late on but that was us finished. When the whistle went we just slumped into the mud. As I trudged off, Spurs keeper Pat Jennings ran over to see me and told me what a great game I had had, but I was in my own little world, as were the rest of the team.

We all got on the bus to leave and there were still City fans outside singing our names. We gave them a wave and thought about what might have been. Looking back, I was voted man of the match in the local press and that was nice, but I still can't help thinking how close we were to getting there and even winning it. Third Division Aston Villa had beaten Manchester United 3–2 in the other semi-final and, although Spurs went on to win the trophy 2–0, I really would have fancied our chances against Villa in the final, but it was not to be.

We struggled in the league after the League Cup exploits, going nine games without a win, the run eventually ending in March with a 3–0 win at Watford, but the defeat had really knocked the stuffing out of us. So a season that came so close to glory ended up a fight for survival with us eventually finishing fourth from bottom in the league and four points from safety.

I left in 1972 for Gillingham as a young Ray Cashley was coming through the ranks at City and to be fair he was such a good prospect for the club. I had worked closely with Ray in a coaching capacity in training, sometimes working one to one with him. It was the sort of thing keepers needed to do as we never had any sort of goalkeeping coaches back then. It tended to be the goalkeepers looking after themselves. I was really pleased that Ray was able to have such a good career at the club, being part of the promotion team in 1976 that got to Division One. I really liked that sort of thing and always thought about coaching for the future. I also enjoyed my time at Gillingham where I was part of the 1973/74 Division Four promotion team that finished behind Peterborough, but I retired soon after due to a problem with my shoulder.

I returned to Bristol where I still had my family home and got a job as a postman. I loved the job and especially the outdoors, and football became a bit of a hobby as I would go and watch a few local games and even turn out just to keep fit now and then. Then around 1982 I was asked by new Bristol City manager Terry Cooper to come back and work behind the scenes on a part-time basis. It was a real shot in the arm for me. I worked it around my postman job and found myself scouting, working with the youth team and also the reserves. The club had been through a real difficult time in the early eighties and nearly went to the wall. We were relying on young lads in the side and behind the scenes we had about five members of staff but we all pulled together. I did eventually get to Wembley as part of the coaching setup when City got to the Freight Rover Final in 1986 and also 1987, which was a great thrill for me. I worked with City on a part-time basis, in the end right up to 2005, as a goalkeeping scout looking at rival keepers and producing reports. I did this until Gary Johnson came in as manager but he had his own people to do that sort of work and I left. I wasn't bitter although I loved being involved. One benefit was that I had Saturdays free and I hadn't had that since I was a kid, so my family benefited.

I look at the club today and they are a million miles away from those days of living hand to mouth, thankfully. They have a fantastic stadium, although I'm sad to see the East End part of the ground go, and they have a forward-thinking owner in Stephen Lansdown and also a young British manager in Lee Johnson who will take them to the Premier League I'm sure in the next few years. Their recent exploits in the League Cup where they beat Manchester United and competed so well against Manchester City in the semi-final certainly brought back some memories of that rainy night at White Hart Lane.

Today I keep myself busy with the family and go to the odd game at Ashton Gate now and again when I have time. The club will always be in my heart and I'm so glad that I can share some memories with the fans in this wonderful book, even if it was a defeat.

LEE JOHNSON

Lee Johnson

Lee Johnson was the epitome of never judging a book by its cover. At first glance this slightly built midfielder looked as though he would struggle in the ball-winning engine room of Bristol City's midfield, but throughout his journey in football this lad from Newmarket has possessed an inner strength and self-belief that has taken him to becoming one of British football's young exciting managers.

After a youth career at Arsenal and Watford the young Johnson took a while to find his feet in the game, stopping at Brighton and Brentford along the way before linking up with his father Gary at Yeovil Town. And it was at Huish Park where he came into his own, achieving two promotions and winning the player of the year award three times in succession. With his stock rising and a thirst to improve himself as a player Johnson signed for Edinburgh giants Heart of Midlothian for £50,000, with things not working out at Hearts, due to their erratic Lithuanian owner Vladimir Romanov. Johnson mulled through various offers and decided to rejoin his father at Ashton Gate. Taking on the calls of nepotism by some sections of fans head on, Johnson flourished in the exciting team his father was putting together. Promotion to the Championship followed in 2006/07 and there was heartbreak the following season as City lost the Championship play-off final, losing 1–0 to Hull City at Wembley. After five and a half years at the club Johnson left in 2012 amassing 174 games and 11 goals in the process. Always a keen student of the game, Johnson had successful manager appointments at Oldham Athletic and Barnsley before getting the call from owner Steve Lansdown to become manager in 2016. Together, both Lansdown and Johnson have turned the club around both on and off the field with the young Johnson becoming one of the top young British coaches in the game.

Bristol City 0 Hull City 1
Championship play-off final
24 May 2008
Wembley Stadium

Bristol City: Basso, Orr, Carey, Fontaine, McAllister, Noble, Elliott, Carle, McIndoe, Adebola, Trundle. Subs: Weale, Vasko, Johnson, Sproule, Byfield.

There are so many different games that come to mind when I look back at my playing days at Bristol City and also my managerial career. But the one that stands out from my playing career may well surprise some fans and that's the Championship play-off final against Hull City in 2008. It was a gut-wrenching defeat for us and I was sub on the day but I learnt so many lessons from it that have stayed with me and have now become invaluable in management. But I will get to that game later.

I suppose I have always had a strong inner belief to back myself when things are not going well; after all, I don't think you could go into football without it. It's a game that will always keep you on your toes and when things are going well you're a king but when they're not you're on your own essentially, and although you have your family and work colleagues around you, it's you who has to summon up that self-belief to get you through.

Like most boys back in the day I always wanted to be a footballer and the estate I was brought up in in Newmarket was brilliant as we would play around it all day until it got dark. Obviously my dad was involved in the game and like most kids you often try to aspire to what your parents are doing. I was originally at Arsenal, and at 15 years old was offered something like a four-year contract, but then Arsene Wenger came in and there were a lot of lads coming in from overseas and I just wasn't getting anywhere.

So I left for Watford who were managed by Graham Taylor. I then had spells at Brighton and Hove Albion and Brentford before going to Yeovil Town. I wasn't really looking to join my dad at Huish Park; in fact, I was already being lined up to go to Denmark and sign for a club and I just went to Yeovil to keep myself fit until the deal happened. Anyway, I loved it there. They were such a good bunch of lads – we went everywhere together. We were like a massive family and that created such a tremendous team spirit within the side that we felt we could beat anyone; we always had each other's backs. Lads like Terry Skiverton and Darren Way were top draw. We enjoyed some success at the club winning two promotions and an FA Trophy. The fans were brilliant – they treated us like the Beatles when we were out in the town. But I felt that maybe the time was right to move on and no disrespect to Yeovil but I wanted to test myself on a bigger platform.

So when I got the chance to go to Hearts it was an opportunity not to be missed. I could have stayed at Yeovil but this was a chance to play in a different league and also of European football. I was signed by manager Graham Rix for £50,000 and the Hearts team at the time were a really good side, proving it on my debut in the Edinburgh derby where we beat Hibernian 4–1 in what was a fantastic game in terms of result for us and atmosphere. I thought, wow this is why I signed. Now I knew the Hearts owner Vladimir Romanov was probably not the most level-headed of owners but things went from bad to worse. He started to pick the team and undermined manager Rix all the time. In the end it became a real shame, which was unfortunate as the side we had were really talented and with a decent owner on board could potentially have taken the team past the likes of Celtic and Rangers.

In the end it was inevitable that I was going to leave, so I had some offers on the table, the main ones being Bristol City and Blackpool. Blackpool, who were in Division One with City, had offered to make me their highest-paid player which was flattering but it has never ever been about the money; it's about the football and where myself and my family would be happiest. I never dealt with my dad during the negotiations; it was purely with Stephen Lansdown, which made things easy for me as I knew there would be a certain section of the fans that would think I was only here due to my dad. So Bristol City was not really the easy choice for me but in terms of football I knew it would be and I loved a challenge. The club were going places. When I signed they had some great lads in the dressing room and we had a really good side with Adriano Basso in goal, the likes of Louis Carey, who was so well organised, in defence, along with Bradley Orr and Jamie McAllister, who would tackle anything that moved, and Alex Russell and David Noble, who would always carve a chance from somewhere.

I do remember one game which I think was my debut at Ashton Gate. It was the fourth game of the season and we had won the opening match against Scunthorpe, but were coming off the back of two away defeats and supporters were not happy, particularly when we lost 4–2 to, ironically, Blackpool who had not gained a point all season. I remember coming off the pitch to the boos and some fan got on the pitch and tried to take a swipe at me saying 'we don't want you or your dad here', which sort of concentrated the mind a bit. Despite the poor start we certainly turned things round that season, finishing second in the league to Scunthorpe and winning promotion. One particular game from that campaign was in the FA Cup against Premiership side Middlesbrough where we were 2–0 down early on at Ashton Gate and turned things round to finish 2–2. I remember hitting a good ball into the box for Richard Keogh to make it 2–1, then Scott Murray lobbing the keeper to level the game. The crowd were amazing that day; you would have thought we had won the game but it showed how strong we were in terms of team spirit. It was a fantastic season for us as we were young lads and to go up was absolutely thrilling. The fans on that final game at home to Rotherham United were incredible; it was a real promotion party and we couldn't get enough of it.

The following season, that determination that we had in games to never give up, saw us in great shape as we became one of the surprise packages of the Championship, although I struggled with injury throughout the campaign and spent a bit of time on the bench. We added one or two players but we were essentially the same side that had come up from Division

One the season before. That determination served us well as many a time that season we would score late on to win matches or draw games we were losing, but we didn't score many in the season to be honest. That never-say-die attitude took us all the way to the play-off semi-final against Crystal Palace. I remember I came off the bench in the second match. I still think the media were waiting for us to fall away as ourselves and Hull City were the surprise packages of the season. The first leg at Palace was fantastic with us winning 2–1 with a very late winner from David Noble giving us the edge, but the home game in the second leg was incredible. They scored to make it 1–1 and put the game into extra time, and we managed to score twice in extra time through Lee Trundle and Michael McIndoe. The scenes at Ashton Gate were crazy. The whole crowd emptied on to the field and the whole place was rocking. I don't think people could believe we were one step away from the Premier League.

And so to the 'Match of my Life'. As I said early on, the play-off final will stay with me for a long time as I learnt many things from that day that have helped me in my career today. From the moment we beat Palace, all eyes were on us and Hull City in terms of both local and national media; after all, the Championship play-off final is supposed to be the richest game in the world, rumoured to be worth £120m to the winner, and that's what makes it so incredible as nobody really remembers the losers and they walk away with nothing. The media interest was full-on with rounds of interviews for us and stories of fans travelling from all corners of the world to see Bristol City's biggest ever match. The pressure was building with every day that went by. I just absorbed it and was desperate to be included in the starting line-up as my ankle had healed weeks ago, and although I had come on in games I really wanted the full 90 minutes, especially at Wembley. I had played against Hull in the two league games against them, the 0–0 draw at the KC Stadium and our 2–1 win at Ashton Gate, so I knew this was going to be a very tight affair. I also remember Dad giving an interview the day before the final to the *Bristol Evening Post* where he pointed out that we were lads with a point to prove. Many of us had been let go by Premier League clubs and this was our chance to prove we were good enough. It was true: myself and David Noble were released from Arsenal, Lee Trundle was shown the door by Everton, Bradley Orr was rejected by Newcastle United and Darren Byfield was let go at Aston Villa.

I received the first bit of disappointing news when I found out I was to be on the bench. I was gutted but I was still part of things. Then we found out just before the game that Jamie McCombe was ill. The omens were bad as Jamie was never ill. Things just didn't seem right on the day; we appeared to be a bit fractious and individual instead of the strong unit that we had been all season. The City fans were incredible as we walked out. They were a sea of red and white and this just filled me with a desire to do it for them. We started well and we knew that they would sit eight men behind the ball, so we needed to be creative and open them up. We had two glorious chances before Hull even got out of the blocks. A lovely ball was played by Marvin Elliott and Dele Adebola managed to hold off the defender but he just managed to toe-poke it to the Hull keeper. Then Nick Carle made some space but shot just wide of the post. We ended up getting punished just before half-time when a ball played into their box was headed back out to Dean Windass, who then headed the ball to Nick Barmby, who seemed to carry it for an age. Windass pushed out to the right taking defenders with him and the young Fraizer Campbell went left; Barmby pushed it to Campbell who was just about to be tackled by Louis Carey but he slipped. Campbell pulled the ball back to Dean Windass who volleyed it into the net giving Basso no chance. It was a disappointing goal to concede as five of us had tracked back but nobody had picked up Barmby or Windass.

There was a shift of power after Bradley Orr went off with a depressed fracture of the cheek after a run-in with Nick Barmby. I came on to occupy the right side of the midfield as we continued to look for an equaliser but we just never created anything. It seemed that the one thing that had got us here, that never-say-die attitude, was missing. I remember Lee Trundle having a great chance from six yards out with minutes to go but stuck it over the bar. With that the whistle went and Wembley went mad in black and gold. Our dream was over as we all slumped to our knees.

On reflection we had a brilliant season but just did not do ourselves justice when it mattered. Hull went up with West Brom and Stoke City and we were destined for another season in the Championship. We just never had that one thing you need and that was an out-and-out goalscorer, somebody clinical in the box like they had with Dean Windass and Fraizer Campbell. Our leading scorer that season was Darren Byfield with eight goals and that was just not good enough. I was gutted for the fans and I could see how hurt Dad was with the defeat, although he tried to pick everybody up. It was something I never forgot and I knew if I ever got in that position again, either as player or manager, that would not happen. It was a defeat that was hard to take, although I always think of that game as a launch pad for me to do things in the future. It was a lesson for the future that I would not forget.

Dad left the club in 2010 by mutual consent and I had really enjoyed my time working with him. He created the type of team spirit that we had at Yeovil Town. Looking back, I think Dad struggled with what was essentially a 'rich' dressing room, and by that I mean there were millionaires sat alongside each other and that can be very difficult to manage. It's very difficult to build team spirit and togetherness in sides where players don't really socialise and come from different cultures, but that is the modern game. I remember a Championship manager saying to me recently that he told a particular player to play in a particular position to which the player replied emphatically, 'No, I am going to be at this club longer than you.' I always thought Dad got the best out of players that were hungry and were not comfortable as such.

I was in and out of the side through injury when Keith Millen took over the reins as manager and I was starting to have niggling trouble with my ankle that had caused me problems from years ago in a tackle with Watford's Danny Shittu. I felt stale at City and I left by mutual consent in 2012. I loved my time at the club and I had made some great friends on and off the field in Bristol. Again I had offers and I went back to Scotland to play for Kilmarnock. Again I enjoyed it, winning the Scottish Cup after beating Celtic 1–0 in the final. But with the ankle playing up I only had a season there.

I was always keen to try management and I went off to learn my trade as it were. I had already done my badges and I travelled across Europe going to see different matches and pick the brains of some of the game's top coaches. I met various knowledgeable people at the start of my management career, all of whom offered a lot of support, such as Kenny Dalglish and Brian Marwood, who is the football administrator at Manchester City, along with Bristol City owner Stephen Lansdown. I sought advice and picked their brains. The chance came in 2013 with Oldham Athletic. They were struggling at the bottom of the league and their owner Simon Corney took a real chance with me as I was young and had no experience, but I knew I could do it; again, it's that self-belief. I remember asking Stephen Lansdown for advice before the interview and he told me they will try and relegate you by saying we want to bring you in but could you work under somebody. To be honest I would have accepted that but Stephen told me to tell them no if you believe in yourself, which I always have. So I told them no and got the job.

It was really backs-to-the-wall stuff. We had some good lads and the job was constant pressure. I remember us playing Mansfield in the FA Cup and if we beat them we were due to play Liverpool at Anfield in the next round. Simon came to see me and told me that we have to beat Mansfield as the Liverpool game will earn us £450,000 and without that people at the club will not get paid. I think that was the biggest pressure I have ever felt in management knowing how other people's lives and futures depended on a result. Anyway, we won and went to Anfield.

I kept Oldham up that year and I even had the chance of pitting my wits against my dad who had gone back to Yeovil as manager. Fortunately for me we beat them 1–0, which was great for us but stalled Yeovil's promotion campaign, but they eventually went up via the play-offs. I had success in the transfer market, selling players for good money and replacing them with bargain buys. I also played some good entertaining football which I suppose led to Barnsley's interest in me.

I left Oldham in 2015 with them ninth in League One and started a new chapter in Barnsley. Again there was a degree of success as we won the Football League Trophy at Wembley beating Oxford United. But I left in February 2016 after a call from Stephen Lansdown to take over at Ashton Gate. I think the offer came as a surprise to some fans and I know a small section were not happy with my appointment, but I have that belief in my own ability and knew I could do well at the club. To become manager at the club was a real thrill and it was exciting to be involved with the plans that Stephen Lansdown had for the club on and off the pitch moving forward into the future. Bristol City were not in a great position in the league when I joined but then that's the reality of football – rarely do you join a club on the up as a manager. We won seven of our final 16 games which meant we were safe in the league. The following season I brought in various players but ended in a relegation dogfight finishing 17th, one place above the previous season.

Obviously if I'm allowed to have a 'Match of my Life' during my time in charge of the club it would have to be a case of 'Matches Of My Life'. The League Cup run was brilliant for us as a side and great for the supporters. We had beaten Premier League opposition along the way to the quarter-finals and we were playing some great football. We had lads who were fit, doing their job intelligently and responsibly, and again a team spirit and inner belief that meant we were a match for anyone.

The game against Manchester United was incredible. We as coaches talked about how we were going to go about this. We decided to play two false number nines as we knew their back four would not come out in the game. This would give us more possession and I knew Paul Pogba was not going to run around Ashton Gate all evening looking for the ball. I viewed the game as a real club day for the fans and it was great to showcase the club and the city of Bristol on the global stage. Obviously with Mourinho coming I had to get a decent bottle of red wine in for after, which we did. The game plan worked a treat and I was really proud of my players and staff throughout the game. To have beaten them like we did put a real marker down on what this club could achieve. You also have to remember Jose put out a very strong side that night which just added to our pride. You could see my delight at the end as I hugged and span around a ball boy.

Jose and I talked at length after the game and he was very knowledgeable about our players, the team and the city of Bristol. I asked him various questions about handling top players and he told me how we deserved the win. I realised then that his private persona is very different from that shown through the media. This was evident when he went on television minutes later and said we were lucky – I did laugh at that. So we had to wait in the tunnel along with the media while the semi-final draw was made, so they could get an instant reaction. I secretly wanted Arsenal as I felt they wouldn't put out a strong team in the first leg and we would exploit that. In the end it was Manchester City and again it meant two fantastic games that showed off my players, the club and the city of Bristol.

After the game I went home and poured myself a whisky and coke and just sat on the settee with my wife and thought, wow, did that just happen? I didn't sleep much as the adrenalin was still buzzing around my body. Next day I remember having a meeting with the coaching staff and people thought I was mad to go to the Etihad and play a 4–4–2 system; they thought they would destroy us. But I had belief in myself, my staff and the players that we could really go and give them a game. But for the time being we had to forget about the cup and crack on with the league, so again football can keep you on your toes.

We went 4–4–2 at the Etihad and gave them a real scare, going 1–0 up through Bobby Reid, and in the end although they won 2–1, we were still in the tie and had given them a real game. Pep Guardiola was different class. We talked after the game and he was interested in how we had approached them with no apparent fear – he was looking for any sort of weakness in his side. I told him we would speak more after the second leg as I didn't want to give him too much info. Again the second leg was great for Bristol. The crowd were unbelievable and although we came so close, losing 3–2 in the end, we had played really well and won a lot of fans with our pressing game. In fact, days later I had around four or five different Premier League sides contact me on what was the best way to play against Manchester City.

Unfortunately our form dipped towards the end of the Christmas period, which to be honest was no real surprise as ten of the side needed operations. We had given so much in the first part of the season and we just never had the depth of squad to cope. I have always had an aim for the club and I feel that we are improving with every season. Obviously we are in the results business and I understand that, but if you look at successful teams over the years nothing worthwhile ever gets built through successful sackings of managers. I would love to have 11 Bristol lads in the side playing top-flight football and, although that may seem naive, I have always kept a path open for any lad coming through from the youth-team system to have a crack at the first team. We play in a very competitive league, arguably the third toughest league in the world, and the clubs around us can double, treble and even quadruple players' wages that we pay, so it's a fine line between being successful and producing our own players. I have always instilled in my sides to stay humble and honest and I think we have always shown that. I see my role at Bristol City as a long-term project and it would be a personal ambition to take this club that I love into the Premier League in the future.

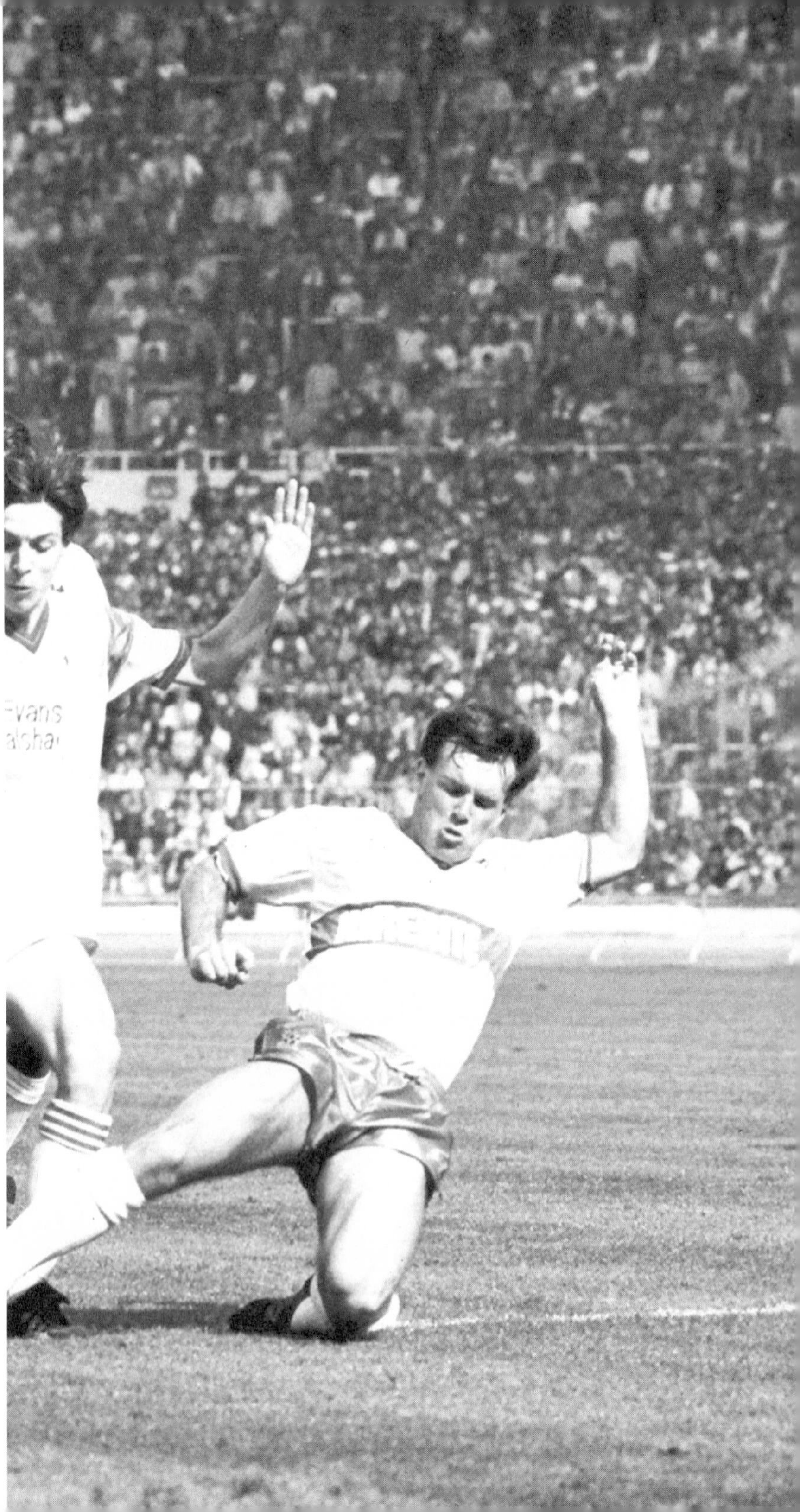

Andy Llewellyn

Andy Llewellyn was your typical no-nonsense defender. He may well not have had the skills or attacking prowess of some of his team-mates, but this tough-tackling, passionate lad from Bristol was Bristol City through and through. Courted by many of the country's top clubs as a youngster, it was only ever going to be Bristol City that captured his signature. Llewellyn's early start in the game coincided with the club's own fall from grace, as when he signed as a schoolboy they were in the dizzy heights of the First Division, yet when he made his debut at 16 the club were bottom of Division Four. The near collapse of the club in 1982 proved to be the launch pad for this loyal City servant to spend 12 years with the club. Andy eventually left his beloved City after being deemed surplus to requirements by manager Russell Osman in 1994. After spells with Exeter City and Hereford United, Llewellyn decided to hang up his boots full time. He will never be forgotten and will always be regarded as one of Bristol City's greatest full-backs.

Bristol City 1 Bristol Rovers 0
Football League Division Two
5 March 1991
Ashton Gate

Bristol City: Leaning, Llewellyn, Bryant, Aizlewood, Scott, May, Shelton, Newman, Donowa, Taylor, Morgan. Subs: Allison, Rennie.

Goal: Donowa.

My god, I really do have an awful lot of games that I could pick for the 'Match of my Life'. I just seem to have played in some of City's great matches over the years and that's something I am extremely proud of. I joined the club as a schoolboy after interest from Bristol Rovers, Aston Villa and Manchester United, but I just wanted to play for City and in hindsight it was the best thing I ever did as I really was thrown into the deep end.

As is well documented, the club were spiralling down the leagues and manager Terry Cooper only had about 20 players to choose from, and this included myself and four other apprentices, so we really were down to bare bones as it were. Terry told me that I was going to travel with the first team away to Rochdale and I was overjoyed just to be travelling with them. When we got there he told me I was playing. I really couldn't believe it that I was making my debut at 16 but I relished the chance to play. The game was a bit of a blur but I will never forget the feeling. We lost 1–0 but Terry was full of praise for me. He picked me the following week against Chester where we lost 1–0 and found ourselves bottom of Division Four. The club were really up against it and I remember us getting Chris Garland to come out of retirement and help out in the team.

There was one particular game where we went to Hereford away on a Tuesday night; we were bottom of the league and all the supporters went in fancy dress. We picked Chris Garland up from Chepstow Races on the way and Chris was in great spirits as he had a few winners that day. The club won 3–1 and it sparked a real turnaround in our fortunes as we picked up some results and finally finished the season mid-table.

When I look back on those early years, for me I cannot speak highly enough of Terry Cooper. He was a manager who had seen it all and done it all in the game with Leeds United and England and was one of the game's greatest full-backs. He was so influential on my career that I would not have been a player if not for him. He worked tirelessly with me, giving me advice and working with me one to one. He used to take me to the club's car park where there were two double wooden doors and he would make me chip the ball against the doors constantly over and over.

After being in the team for a bit he took me out of the side for a break but he still involved me. Then we were going to play away at Stockport and he told me I was travelling with the side. I warmed up with them before kick-off and just before we went out on the pitch he asked me in a crowded dressing room whether I would like to play tonight. Obviously, I said yes. He told me I would need to be more vocal in my play, and with that he got me to stand on the bench seat that was in the changing room and shout as loud as I could all the things that I would be doing in tonight's game. I was really embarrassed as all the senior players like John Shaw, Glyn Riley and Tom Ritchie were laughing. So I shouted 'Referee', 'Hold it', 'Man on', 'Offside', that sort of thing. When I was finished, Terry and the lads applauded me and told me that's what you do to help your team-mates. It really did me the world of good in terms of confidence.

Although he did cause me some heartache sometimes, like when we got to Wembley in the Freight Rover Final against Bolton Wanderers. I was sub for the game and was really gutted as it was every player's dream to play at Wembley. The day was brilliant for the club as there were about 40,000 City fans there and they had the time of their lives. The team did brilliantly that day, outplaying Bolton. We were 3–0 up and I was sat on the bench just shouting at Terry 'Let me on, let me on'. But he kept saying 'in a minute' or 'Run up the touchline'. This went on and on and in the end the ref blew the whistle and I never got on. Looking back, I just think Terry was so wrapped up in the game he genuinely forgot. I was devastated. He threw his arms around me after and said, 'You're young enough to come back again.' I, on the other hand, was not so sure. Anyway, in the end, he was right as we came back the following year in the competition but we lost on penalties to Mansfield. He did say to me 'I told you so' after he picked me in the team.

As I said before, Terry was a massive influence on me and he is a very clever man who had total belief in himself. I remember he brought Joe Jordan to the club and he had one eye on Joe becoming his successor. I really can't think of many football managers who would be planning their successor, but Terry did. This shows that he was not worried that Joe would undermine him – he knew Joe would be a perfect fit. He was right because, when Terry left, the board turned to Joe who again was a great manager and one who helped me greatly on and off the field. We called him gaffer straightaway and he had the total respect of everyone. Whenever we went to hotels you could see the people in the foyers stop when they saw him. It gave us all a lift as we walked behind him.

My career at City has involved promotions, relegations and cup wins, but throughout all of it, my one 'Match of my Life' has to be a game against local rivals Bristol Rovers. The derby games with those north of the river have always been very special affairs. They give the fans bragging rights and it always brings an incredible atmosphere to the games. You have to remember City and Rovers split work colleagues and even families in terms of support and it's a massive game in the city. Although lately those games are now few and far between with both clubs being so far away in terms of league position. My game in 1991 was incredible in terms of rivalry. We didn't have a great record against Rovers in the league and it was a long time since we had beaten them, so we really owed it to the supporters to put on a display. In the build-up there was not much between us as we lay one point ahead of them in the league. The local press were obviously building the game up, so by the time around 22,000 were packed into Ashton Gate it was very much game on.

I remember before the match there was a minute's silence for our chairman Des Williams who had died of a heart attack ten days earlier. Everybody from the club, backroom staff and alike, all gathered on the edge of the pitch. Unfortunately there were a few jeers from some of the Rovers fans during the silence, and from the pitch we could see that the Williams family were very upset by it and that just added to our determination to do well.

We got at Rovers right from the start and there were a few tasty tackles put in on both sides. I think the ref knew he was in for a tough game that night. We had some good early chances with Nicky Morgan and Bob Taylor going close. Louie Donowa, our recent purchase from Ipswich Town, was only playing due to Dave Smith being out injured with a thigh strain, but Louie was giving the Rovers defence a torrid time out on the flanks. The City fans had really not seen the best of Louie since his £45,000 move but he was certainly showing them he was worth every penny. Whenever I got the ball he would be screaming for me to give it to him. Rovers sat back and just absorbed the pressure, looking for a chance to hit us on the break. I gave the ball away at one point and Ian Holloway put a ball through for Devon White, but he just stuck the ball wide as I had my heart in my mouth.

We were defending the old open end at Ashton Gate and it was packed with Rovers fans who were giving us stick all game. We really piled on the pressure and had most of the chances during the first half. I got into a bit of a scuffle with Rovers forward Cal Saunders and we ended up pushing each other before the ref split us up. Just before half-time I clattered into Rovers winger Tony Pounder and the ref booked me and told me to behave myself. We went in at half-time level and our manager Jimmy Lumsden just kept telling us that we were the better side and chances would come.

In the second half we started where we had left off, getting right at them. Gary Shelton was imposing his authority on Ian Holloway in the midfield and he was driving us on. Nicky Morgan hit the Rovers post with a great effort and I was thinking we will score soon. Then with about 15 minutes to go Mark Aizlewood played a terrible back pass to keeper Andy Leaning and Rovers frontman Devon White latched straight on to it and was brought down by Leaning and the ref gave a penalty. I couldn't believe it and I'm sure I shouted a few choice words in the direction of Aizlewood about the back pass. The penalty was in front of our supporters in the East End and Rovers midfielder Ian Holloway stepped up to take it. He hit it towards Andy's left and Andy managed to get his hands to it and save it. We rushed towards him to congratulate him as the fans went wild. Andy just pushed us away and told us to get on with the game. The noise the City fans were making was deafening; it was as though we had scored. Rovers seemed shell-shocked, as though they knew that was their chance.

With minutes left, Matt Bryant hit a free kick up front and Wayne Allison flicked it on for Louie Donowa who hit the ball against the oncoming Rovers keeper Brian Parkin. The ball bounced off Parkin and back to Louie who headed the ball into the net and Ashton Gate erupted. We were in front of the Rovers fans and we milked every moment of it, much to their annoyance. Then as the police started to walk around the edge of the pitch we knew the ref was going to blow soon and then he did. We celebrated like we had won promotion; it was the first time we had beaten them in five years and we were going to enjoy it. We celebrated in the changing room and then a few of us went out for a drink after the game.

In the morning I got a call from manager Jimmy Lumsden who told me to get myself to the ground as soon as possible. I asked him what it was about but he just said he would tell me when I got there. When I got to the ground skipper Rob Newman was also there with Jimmy who did not look happy. He told me that Avon and Somerset police wanted to speak to me and Rob about an incident last night. We went to Broadbury Road police station and were interviewed separately. The officer asked me where I was last night around 9.45. And what I was doing. I really thought it was a wind-up as I told them I was at Ashton Gate playing football and 22,000 people could vouch for me. The officer told me that a complaint had been made about alleged obscene gestures made by myself and Rob towards Rovers fans at last night's game after the City goal.

In the end the complaint was dropped by the police but we had to go before the FA later in the year. When the date for the hearing arrived, myself, Rob and striker Bob Taylor had to cut a City tour abroad short so we could attend. Bob apparently was accused of making a gesture with his hand, but in fairness to him it was a gesture he made every time he scored. After the hearing myself and Rob were found not guilty but poor old Bob was found guilty and had to pay a fine. He was absolutely livid on the way home, which did make me and Rob laugh. We later found out that the complaint was made to the police by two Rovers fans and that was the last we heard of the matter. When I look back it really was an incredible memory of a Bristol derby and certainly the one game I will never forget for what happened both on and off the pitch.

I continued my time at City and things were still going well. Jimmy had left, I saw Denis Smith come and go as manager and then Russell Osman took over. Again there was that famous night under Russell where we beat Liverpool at Anfield in a match I will never forget. But my time was coming to an end as far as Russell was concerned. Although I was still playing well, Russell pulled me to one side and told me that the club would not be renewing my contract at the end of the season. He believed that they had a right-back at the club called Marvin Harriott who would take my place in the coming season, and Russell thought so highly of him that he told me he would go on and play for England. No disrespect to Marvin but I knew that was not going to happen.

In the end, I left the club. I had a few offers and chose to go down to Exeter City, but to be honest my heart just wasn't in it. I played a season there and then turned out for Hereford United and Yeovil Town before hanging up my boots. City gave me a testimonial against Manchester United which was fantastic as loads of players who I played with turned out to honour me – players like Joe Jordan, Alan Walsh, Andy Cole and Dariusz Dziekanowski – so it was really emotional for me and something that I will never forget. The fans were amazing that night and to be honest they always have been with me, even today. I think they know how much the club means to me and always will.

GEOFF MERRICK

Geoff Merrick

Legend is a term that is frequently banded about when it comes to footballers but when it comes to Geoff Merrick no truer word has been spoken. Throughout his time at Ashton Gate he had been at the very centre of the club's greatest highs, such as promotion to Division One, and the deep despair of 1982 when he and seven other players ripped up their contracts to save the club. A cultured footballer, from an early age this local lad was pursued by the country's elite clubs but the young Merrick chose to sign for his local club City. He made his debut at 17 years of age and it was manager Alan Dicks who nurtured him into becoming the club's captain at the age of 20. At the helm of a young City side, Merrick's greatest triumph was the promotion to Division One in 1976. Again he came to the attention of many top clubs, including Arsenal who it's rumoured had tabled a bid of £300,000 for the defender, but the club rejected it and Merrick was not allowed to speak to the Gunners. Many feel a move to Arsenal may have paved the way for the young lad from Ashton to have gone on to play for England, but we will never know. After four years in the top flight, the club descended into chaos with Merrick and seven fellow players given the ultimatum of tearing up their contracts to save the club. This they did and Merrick left City to go and play abroad for the remainder of his career before returning to the south-west to play non-league football. Merrick will always be remembered as a fantastic servant to Bristol City on and off the pitch.

Leeds United 0 Bristol City 1
FA Cup fifth round replay
19 February 1974
Elland Road

Bristol City: Cashley, Sweeney, Drysdale, Gow, Collier, Merrick, Tainton, Ritchie, Fear, Gillies, Hunt. Sub: Rodgers.

Goal: Gillies.

Fans may be surprised by my choice of 'Match of my Life'; after all, I was there at some of the club's greatest moments. The night we won promotion against Portsmouth and leading the club out on that sunny afternoon against Arsenal at Highbury will always be special to me and also really important in the club's history. But for me personally it has to be the two games against Leeds United in the FA Cup, and in particular the win at Elland Road.

We were a bunch of lads on the verge of something special and that proved to be true as we gained promotion two years later with more or less the same team. The Leeds game, I felt, was when people stood up and took notice of us and thought that maybe we could achieve something with this group of players. It was also a fantastic achievement as Leeds United were the best team in Britain and possibly Europe at the time with 11 internationals in the side, and to go to their own backyard and beat them will always be a special memory for me.

I think it's well documented that Bristol City were my club. I used to go and see them when I was a kid with my dad; one of my earliest memories is of us walking to the games together. I trained with them but they did take their time in offering me the chance to sign for them. I had played five times for England Schoolboys at under-15 level – they were two games against West Germany, matches against Scotland and Northern Ireland and one against Wales, which was at Ashton Gate. As I said, I had been training with City, but nothing was offered, so I had registered at Soundwell College in Bristol to become a painter and decorator. But then City manager Fred Ford came to my house and asked me to sign, which I did.

It was a real dream being at the club and I remember meeting the great John Atyeo which was a real thrill for me. The changing room was a tough old place as manager Fred Ford took no prisoners and there were some seasoned professionals in there at the time, like Mike Gibson, Ken Wimshurst, Jack Connor and Alec Briggs, whilst also having a few youngsters like Chris Garland and Jantzen Derrick. My debut was towards the end of the season away at Aston Villa. We were close to relegation but our results had picked up and we were safe, so I think that's why Fred put me in. It was a great occasion for me, especially with us coming out 4–2 winners.

There was upheaval during the summer as Fred Ford left and Alan Dicks joined as manager and I became very much part of his dream for Bristol City in the future. Alan was a decent bloke – we didn't see eye to eye all of the time but he made me captain when I was 20 and that made me feel ten feet tall. I remember him calling me into his office to tell me, and at the time I was the youngest captain in all four divisions. As a team we struggled for three or four years, dicing with relegation, before Alan got rid of some of the older lads and brought in a new younger set who were local as well as a few golden nuggets from Scotland like Gerry Gow, Donnie Gillies, Gerry Sweeney and Tom Ritchie. We had a fantastic team spirit and we just seemed to grow together as players and friends.

I remember getting the draw against Leeds United. We were coming back from a game against Hereford United and had stopped for something to eat in the Wye Valley. The radio was on in the coach and when Leeds United at home came out we just jumped up and down. Leeds, along with Liverpool, were the biggest team in the country at the time and the whole side was full of internationals. The whole of the city was buzzing with the thought of Leeds coming to Ashton Gate and there was a rush on for us to get tickets for friends and relations. It seemed every paper, both locally and nationally, wanted an interview, and as captain I was the one who was pushed in front of the camera.

The game at Ashton Gate was, as expected, a full house – I even think there were people locked out. We played really well and although we went 1–0 down in the first half with a Billy Bremner goal, we matched them man for man and got our reward in the second half when Keith Fear popped up to draw us level. The whole of Ashton Gate was bouncing around and when the whistle went we did think that maybe we had missed our chance. After all, Leeds United had not been beaten for about 30 games so the odds were now firmly stacked against us getting a result up at Elland Road. Thinking about it, the fact that people thought we had missed our chance probably made us more relaxed, as we had nothing to lose.

We went up the day before and the game was a 2pm kick-off on a Wednesday afternoon because there was a miners' strike on and that affected national power supplies, so there would be no floodlights. It's incredible to think that the game was a full house with people even locked out of the ground. I can't begin to think of how many Bristol City fans pulled sickies that day to go to the game. I know there were thousands of red and white scarves there; apparently 8,000 City fans had travelled north on a Wednesday afternoon, which is incredible.

We knew Leeds were going to come at us, especially in front of their own fans, and the opening 30 minutes were really backs to the wall for us. I don't think we had that many chances as they continued to bombard our goal. Manager Alan Dicks told us to not give them any space as they would hurt us and to a man we ran ourselves ragged, pressuring them and hustling them. It worked and we went in at half-time all square at 0–0. When we got to the dressing room, manager Alan Dicks and his assistant John Sillett were telling us how well we had done. I remember midfielder Trevor Tainton having a problem with his hamstring but physio Les Bardsley strapped him up so he wouldn't have to come off.

The second half was the same as the first. Leeds were on top, but me, Gary Collier and Brian Drysdale had done a great job on the Leeds front three of Peter Lorimer, Allan Clarke and Mick Jones, and as for Gerry

Gow, he was matching Billy Bremner in the midfield. As the game went on, the Leeds fans started to get on the Yorkshire men's backs and on 73 minutes the unthinkable happened. Gerry Gow, who was easily the man of the match, cut out a ball from Bremner which he gave to Keith Fear. Keith played a lovely ball into some open space on the edge of the Leeds box and Donnie Gillies ran on to it chased by Norman Hunter. Donnie outmuscled Hunter and slipped the ball past the oncoming Harvey in the Leeds goal. We were ecstatic and they looked like the wind had been kicked out of them. We hung on till the end and when the final whistle blew I was overcome with emotion, so I grabbed the nearest person to me, which happened to be referee Jack Taylor, who didn't have the greatest reputation as a happy figure. Anyway, I grabbed him and ruffled his hair in delight. He looked at me and I thought he was going to book me but he just walked away as I joined the rest of the team.

The dressing room after was as if we had won the cup. It was an incredible achievement, looking back. We were a mid-table Second Division side and they were top of the First Division and had 11 internationals in the squad that day, and internationals who have gone on to be legends in the game. It's a day I won't forget in a hurry. I also remember Liverpool manager Bill Shankly coming into the dressing room to congratulate us and wish us well. They were to be our next opponents and we gave him some banter about how we were going to knock them out as well which he enjoyed.

When Liverpool came to town it was incredible for us and the fans. I had a problem with my ankle and I left it until the morning of the match to have a fitness test on it. I was desperate to play but I knew deep down it wasn't right and I didn't want to let the team and myself down by being selfish and saying it was okay. So I told Alan Dicks that I couldn't play. Looking back, it was a really tough decision for me to make. Dave Rodgers came in to take my place and again we gave them a really good game, but ended up losing 1–0 through a John Toshack goal. I hated watching from the sidelines but I was really proud of the lads and the supporters who cheered all game.

As I said, those games really gave us a taste for the big matches, and that season we finished in the lower half of the table but we were determined to give it everything the following season, which we did by finishing fifth, which was incredible for us. After that we eventually got promotion to Division One and I could not have been prouder to be a Bristol boy leading my local club into the top flight.

Much was made regarding interest from Arsenal but if I'm honest I never wanted to go there as I was happy where I was. I thought about it and at the end of the day I was captain and playing every week which may not have been the case at Highbury. So I was pleased when the club refused me permission to talk to them. Much has been made of my eventual departure from the club, and I know a lot of supporters have different views about it and many don't even know it happened, but it was something that if I'm honest I have never really got over.

The club were in a complete nosedive; we had fallen through the leagues and things were rumbling around the place. We played a reserve game away at Aston Villa and, when we returned, our midfielder Jimmy Mann was waiting for us with a scruffy old bit of paper that he had been given by the directors with names on. We were told to report to the club the following morning without any explanation. When I look back, the scrap bit of paper really symbolises how the whole affair was handled. It was shoddy – the directors couldn't even tell us face to face. I and seven others were told by one of the directors that we had to rip up our contracts in order to save the club. We all had existing contracts and mine had two years left on it, but the club could pay me 14 pence in the pound out of what it was worth. We were put under enormous pressure by the club and the media, and although we called in the PFA chairman Gordon Taylor he wasn't much use as this had not happened before. We said we would play for less money in order to stay but the club wanted to clear its debts and start again. Looking back, I love this club and I'm glad they survived, but the way they did it was scandalous. I felt as though I had been abandoned by them. I, like the rest of the lads, had to sink or swim. I even turned out for the reserves days later and that was my last appearance for Bristol City at Ashton Gate in front of 100 people. It really wasn't the way I wanted to finish – it was dreadful.

Chris Garland and I went to play in Hong Kong but it was out of necessity as there were only a few offers and I needed to look after my family. The club organised a benefit game for us – Southampton v Ipswich Town – which I couldn't attend due to me being away but it wasn't very well promoted, and I think only about 4,000 turned up. People may say I'm bitter but I think what hurts is that from the moment I left that day nobody from the club ever contacted me and asked 'How are you, Geoff?', and that is very difficult to take.

I left Hong Kong after a couple of months and went and played part-time football locally whilst trying various jobs like working on a farm and window cleaning. In the end I became a very successful builder around the south-west, which I'm very proud of. I have said it before: I love the club, and the supporters have always been incredible to me whenever we meet. I wish them all the success in the future but they are not the Bristol City I knew and loved all those years ago when I played in the 'Match of my Life'.

SCOTT MURRAY

Scott Murray

Scott Murray joins a list of illustrious Scotsmen who the Ashton Gate faithful have fallen in love with over the years. Players like Gerry Gow, Tom Ritchie, Donnie Gillies, Gerry Sweeney and Joe Jordan all find themselves imprinted in the very DNA of the club, but they all pale into insignificance compared to the love supporters have for the lad from Aberdeen who found himself at Ashton Gate via a fish factory and the Aston Villa reserves.

Brought to the club by manager John Ward, this Flying Scotsman became a fans' favourite from the off with his speed, skill and match-winning ability. This, combined with his bubbly personality off the field when dealing with supporters, has made him one of the most popular players of his generation. Murray's exploits in his first spell at the club, particularly the 2002/03 season, saw him top scorer at the club with 26 goals. This also brought in a £650,000 bid from highflying Reading, who then captured his services. The pull of Ashton Gate became too much for the young Scot and a season later he was brought home by manager Danny Wilson, much to the City fans' joy. Continuing where he left off, Murray spent a further five seasons at Ashton Gate, before working for the club's commercial department and then becoming the first team's kit man. Murray lived his and many a schoolboy's dream of becoming a professional footballer, but unlike many of today's players he never forgot the chance he had been given. He truly is 'one of our own'.

Cardiff City 1 Bristol City 3
Football League Division Two
29 December 2001
Ninian Park

Bristol City: Stowell, Carey, Hill, Burnell, Coles, Tinnion, Murray, Thorpe, Matthews, Brown, Bell. Subs: Lever, Amankwaah.

Goals: Murray 2, Matthews.

My journey to Bristol City is like that of many young lads. I had a dream to be a professional footballer and at times when I was younger I never thought it would happen, but you have to keep faith in yourself and that is not always easy. I played in the Highland League with Fraserburgh and had a few trials with my local side Aberdeen, as well as Glasgow Rangers and Liverpool, but nothing ever materialised. If I'm honest I was happy playing for Fraserburgh and working in a fish factory driving a forklift truck. I think I thought my chance had gone. Then I was spotted as it were by a manager in the Highland League who had contacts at Aston Villa and I went down for a trial and things went really well. When I signed for Villa I was earning less money than when I was part-time at Fraserburgh and working in the factory, but I had been given my chance. I was told recently that the fee Villa paid for me – £35,000 – was the highest ever paid to a Highland League side, so I'm glad I never had that pressure of knowing that at the time. I coped well at Villa and my only real problem was getting my head round the fact that I was playing with players like Dalian Atkinson and Dwight Yorke after seeing them on the TV. I really was a bit star-struck but they were great players to be around.

Looking back, I probably should have left Villa earlier than I did. I loved it there and made a couple of first-team appearances, but over 200 in the reserves, so maybe I was just really comfortable at the club. I then got chatting to former chairman Doug Ellis and he told me that I was on my way to Bristol City. Apparently City manager John Ward had been watching me in the reserves and they made a bid which Ellis had accepted. I knew nothing of Bristol at the time but when I came down to the club it reminded me of Aberdeen's ground with all the red seats. The dressing room I arrived at was full of young Bristol lads and they really made me feel at home.

The first weekend when I arrived, we all went to a hotel for defender Louis Carey's birthday. Now, I'm a terrible drinker, and centre-forward Colin Cramb took me under his wing and decided that we should all have a drinking game of downing vodka. Wanting to impress, I joined in, not knowing that all the other lads were drinking water whilst I was on vodka. The game ended with me asleep under one of the tables. I play Sunday football with Louis and Colin now and they never let me forget it. So, as you can see, the dressing room was loud and there was a real buzz about the place that I thrived on.

I love this club and its fans; they took me to their hearts the moment I pulled on that red shirt and that's something I will never forget. I am thrilled to be asked to contribute to this great book although my memory is terrible. Even now I get YouTube clips sent to me from fans showing different goals I scored, and I have to look really closely and think, wow, was that me? I have played in some really good talented sides for City over my career and I have shared some great moments like promotions and cup wins; I have also tasted the other side of football like play-off defeats and managers getting the sack, but I suppose that's football.

I have enjoyed looking back over games I have been part of and there are a couple that spring to mind. The goal I scored against Middlesbrough in the FA Cup to make it 2–2 after we were 2–0 down was really special, not only due to the fact that it was on the TV, but I remember it just popped up lovely for me and I just lobbed the keeper. It was a really important time to score as well as we were on a roll and Middlesbrough were under the cosh. The incredible game against Mansfield is also a favourite where we won 5–4 after being 4–2 down. It's a game that was a bit surreal to be honest – it was like playing in a school playground. I remember they had a man sent off and they just thought they had won it, but we never gave up and neither did the fans as they were still singing even when we were losing. We got back in the game and just steamrollered them. I think the winner came in the sixth minute of added time. When the whistle went we just went mental with our travelling fans. It was a really great win, and to cap it all off our manager Danny Wilson made the coach driver stop off at a pub on the way home so we could all have a pint. I have to say that was the only time that ever happened in the whole of my career.

The one game I have picked for 'Match of my Life' has to be the one against Cardiff City in 2001 at Ninian Park. It's a game that I'm always asked about and I truly think it was the one match that brought me closer to the fans. I never really played in a Bristol derby game; I think I played in one and the atmosphere was good but not like this. I think it was due to us and Rovers being in different leagues for most of my career at City. I certainly never realised the passion, and at times hateful atmosphere, of the Severn derby. The clubs are only about 50 miles apart and you have to throw the England versus Wales aspect into the mix along with, at the time, proper old football grounds that were right on top of you – it all added to the experience. Some players hated playing at Ninian Park but I just thrived on the atmosphere.

In the build-up to the game we were both pretty close in terms of league table and Cardiff had won their previous five games at home. They were also bolstered by the signing of former Premier League full-back Dean Gordon from Middlesbrough, so I wasn't really filled with confidence that I was going to have a good game. The crowd were hostile as ever, as they booed all of our names as the team sheet was read out. They also had chairman Sam Hammam walking around the ground tapping his head, a move called the Ayatollah, to get the fans going, and the noise we could hear from the dressing room certainly proved it worked. I was never nervous before games like some players. Tommy Doc used to be sick in the toilet before matches and then go out and have a blinder, whereas I would be just trying to gee people up. As we came out through the tunnel there was a large moose head on the wall for some reason. Sam Hammam tapped it, for good luck I assume, but we just said to each other if we score let's tap our heads as it will wind them up.

We didn't start well and I remember slipping in a massive puddle, much to the joy of the Cardiff fans. They were a really good side and midfielder Graham Kavanagh, who they had signed from Stoke City for £1m earlier in the season, was pulling all the strings in midfield and making them tick. Our talisman Brian Tinnion just could not get hold of the ball and therefore I couldn't get a run at their defence, as it's safe to say Brian always looked for me and I knew a quality ball was on its way. Even today Tinns always says he made 99 per cent of my goals and that's probably true. We were battered first half and the second half was no different. I was also the main focus for the Cardiff fans in the 'Bob Bank', which is where the loudest fans congregate. Every time I got the ball they booed but I really enjoyed it.

Cardiff went 1–0 up through Kavanagh just after half-time and the place erupted. Things got worse for me as I was booked by the ref for arguing over a decision. This just made the Cardiff fans enjoy it even more. Suddenly, about five minutes later, I worked the ball to Tony Thorpe and he put in a wonderful cross that I caught on my chest and ran after. The move completely flustered full-back Dean Gordon and I just raced to put the ball past the keeper. In doing so, I tapped my head, and the travelling City fans went wild and the Cardiff fans just wanted to get at me and kill me. The lads ran to me and congratulated me – they were also laughing over what I had done. When we stood for the kick-off I was getting all sorts of coins thrown at me, which just made me turn to them and smile. Two minutes later we were on the attack again and I received a pass from Aaron Brown on the edge of the box. I just instinctively hit it and it somehow went under the keeper to put us 2–1 up. I just turned and ran in front of the Cardiff fans who were booing me and throwing all sorts of missiles in my direction. With that I cupped my left hand to my ear laughing and skipping as I went. I think I had about £15 bounce off my head in change; they were absolutely livid.

Three minutes later Tony Thorpe picked out Lee Matthews and he put us 3–1 up. It was an amazing turnaround for us and it literally silenced the home crowd, as some of them started to leave the ground. When the final whistle went I have never sprinted so fast towards the tunnel. The game felt like a cup tie and we were jumping about and singing in the dressing room after. We were all buzzing from the result. It will always be one of my highlights in a City shirt as we never really got much at Ninian Park, so to win in the manner we did was incredible. The following season the game was televised and there was a banner in the Cardiff end questioning my parentage which really made me laugh. Games like that don't come along very often so when they do you have to embrace every moment and I certainly did that afternoon at Ninian Park.

My City career went from strength to strength with me scoring regularly for the club. I was aware my agent was looking to get me a move but I had no intention of asking for one as I was really happy at the club. Then a big offer of £650,000 came in from Reading, who were the highflyers in the Championship at the time, and City accepted it. I met Reading manager Alan Pardew and I signed, but I always knew I would be back at some point. Leaving was a real wrench and I described it like the time I left Scotland to come down to Villa – I really felt like I was leaving home. In fact, I bought a house in Hungerford which was an equal distance between Reading and Bristol. Things went well at Reading and they are a decent club, but manager Alan Pardew left for West Ham, new boss Steve Coppell came in and I wasn't in the first team for the first couple of games. That is always an indication that you might not have a future.

I was in the reserves and still scoring and I remember getting two goals on a Tuesday night before transfer deadline day. I was driving home when reserve boss Nicky Hammond rang me and said I had to ring the gaffer. I genuinely thought he was going to say that he was putting me in the side on Saturday, but he said well done on the goals but he had just signed Glen Little in my position and Bristol City had made an offer. It was a no-brainer and I have to say fair play to Steve Coppell as he kept me informed and really didn't have to make that call; I could have found out in the press.

I was delighted when Danny Wilson brought me back for a second spell; it felt like I had not been away. I spent a further five years at the club and had some great times, before hanging up my City boots and going to work in the club's commercial department, whilst turning out for Yeovil Town for a season and Bath City for two. It was while I was at the commercial department that I got a call from the then-manager Derrick McInnis who asked me if I would be interested in becoming the club's new kit man. He said I was such a bubbly person around the place that I would be great in the dressing room with the lads. I thought for a bit and I said I would love to. And that's what I have been doing ever since. I have loved still being part of the football world and I can understand how some players struggle with depression, particularly going from all the adulation to nothing. I love the banter of the place and the club really seems to be going places under Lee Johnson.

I particularly love his philosophy of honesty and basics he has brought to the place, and that is shown with all the young lads going back to cleaning first-team players' boots as we used to back in the day. For me, the kit job is hard work but I have it down to a fine art now, something I certainly struggled with early on when I took everything with me just so I wouldn't forget anything. There was barely room for the players on the coach. My love for this club is well documented and Bristol is my home and always will be. It will be an honour to share my 'Match of my Life' with City fans and I hope my recollections will bring back some memories and shine a light on what the club means to me.

ROB NEWMAN

Rob Newman

Rob Newman was thrown into the Bristol City limelight and never looked back. Whereas some youngsters sink without a trace, Rob established himself as a true City leader. Thrust into the spotlight out of necessity rather than anything else after the Ashton Eight ripped up their contracts in the fallout from the financial mess the club found itself in, this lad from Bradford-on-Avon went on to be a hero to the City fans and to become a shining light during the club's darkest days. Happy to play in a number of roles, Newman earned a reputation of being a jack of all trades during his fledgling career. But it was in central defence that the accomplished Newman found himself at home. With his cultured passing and vision, he progressed to captain, where he led the team to promotion to Division Two in 1990. In total, Newman amassed almost 500 games for the Robins before being transferred to Norwich City for £600,000 in 1991. With the Canaries he played the top-flight football he had always wanted to achieve with Bristol City. Newman played over 200 games for the Canaries before finishing his career with Southend United, where he went on to be manager. After a stint managing Cambridge United and time as assistant manager at Bournemouth, Newman now heads up recruitment and scouting at Manchester City.

Bristol City 0 Fulham 0
Football League Division Three
6 February 1982
Ashton Gate

Bristol City: Moller, Stevens, Hay, Newman, Williams, Nicholls, Musker, Bray, Chandler, Harford, Economou. Sub: Smith.

It's a real honour to be asked to contribute to this book. In my time at City I really did see all the highs and lows of the club. I came to the club as a schoolboy. Southampton were interested in me and they always invited me down to their place for training in the school holidays and City were also interested, but there was nothing really concrete from either clubs until my last year of school when City scout Jock Rae, who was a lovely man and sadly no longer with us, came to my house and asked me to sign schoolboy forms. I was overjoyed but things were by no means nailed on in terms of getting an apprenticeship. When I was old enough, City were taking on 11 apprentices and they had already taken on ten before they got to me. Manager Alan Dicks and his backroom staff of Ken Wimshurst, Gerry Sharpe and Roger Quinton were making the decision and I learnt later that two wanted me and two didn't, but I never found out which way they voted.

Anyway, I got the apprenticeship and then the club literally imploded. With massive debts that had built up over the years, and a certain amount of mismanagement behind the scenes, it was left to eight first-team players to rip up their contracts in order to save the club, which they duly did.

The sacrifice those players made will never be forgotten by myself as it led to me having a career in the game and enabled me to amass so many first-team games as a youngster. The club were really down to bare bones. Alan Dicks had left and we had Bob Houghton take over for a while, but we were literally falling through the divisions.

This takes me to my 'Match of my Life' and it's a game that I will always remember, not only as it was my debut, but also the behind-the-scenes work that was going on, and it really was the start of a new beginning for the club. It was against Fulham who were top of the league. Roy Hodgson was our manager and we were second from bottom in Division Three and destined for Division Four. It was the first game after the Ashton Gate eight had ripped up their contracts and incredibly, as a show of support for us players and the club, many of those players paid to come and watch the match, which shows the dignity they had. I remember seeing striker Chris Garland queue up outside at the turnstile with his two kids to come and watch the match, bearing in mind days before he tore up his contract. That's the quality of the man. As I said, behind the scenes things were frantic. The game almost never went ahead due to a dispute between the old and new companies. Apparently the contract to sign over ownership of the club only happened at 7pm on the Friday night. Directors had paid for the match programmes themselves and also for the drink that was going to be in the directors' lounges and offered to the Fulham board. Supporters had been collecting for the club with buckets and sponsored walks. I will never forget the atmosphere on the day. I also remember most of the backroom people at the club all worked for nothing to get the game on.

I knew I was going to be playing as we only had about 14 players, so I made my debut along with Wayne Bray and Jon Economou, which really was the nucleus of the youth team. The City side really had one player of experience which was keeper Jan Moller, who had played for Sweden in the 1978 World Cup and had been in goal for Malmo in the European Cup Final against Nottingham Forest. God knows what he must have thought, looking back. There were no nerves from us as Roy told us before the game this is a win-win situation for you. Fulham were riding high under manager Malcolm Macdonald and the whole of the City fans didn't expect anything from us, but we knew they were right behind us. Walking out, the crowd were amazing. There were 10,000 in Ashton Gate and it sounded like 50,000; I have never felt so proud. I was playing right-back and it was a position I had never played before, but that was just typical of the day.

We started really well, and in the first couple of minutes Wayne Bray tested the Fulham keeper Gerry Peyton with some fine shots that really lifted us and the crowd. We just kept running and running, hassling Fulham every time they had the ball. I think we were just fearless and certainly were not afraid of the task, even though Fulham had some really good players. I remember Gary Williams, who was playing his first game at centre-back for City, talking the rest of the back four through the game. Then just before half-time, our striker Ricky Chandler had a great chance with a volley that Fulham keeper Peyton pushed along the goal line just out of reach of our other striker Mick Harford. I also had a free kick that just went over the bar. Come half-time we were applauded off the pitch which was an incredible feeling. Roy was overjoyed in the dressing room and although a lot of us were knackered we geed each other up for the second half.

We enjoyed some good moments just after half-time when again Ricky Chandler and Wayne Bray both went close. Fulham never really bothered us until late in the game when Jan Moller showed his quality with some fine saves. With about ten minutes to go I was doubled up with cramp and Roy brought me off. I was replaced with Mark Smith, who was another debutant from the youth team. We hung on in the end, and when the ref blew for the final whistle we all just ran on to the pitch, even me with my cramp. The whole of Ashton Gate stood up on its feet to cheer us off the pitch. It was a great moment for me personally, and the club, as it meant we were back. The press afterwards were great with stories of the heroic display of the Bristol Babes and the supporters were amazing to us. That season we were relegated to Division Four, which was no surprise considering how threadbare the team was.

Life in Division Four became really hard as we found ourselves at the very bottom of the league, but our team spirit was great and also the relationship the supporters had with us; they travelled everywhere to support us. Then, when Roy Hodgson left, the club brought in

Terry Cooper who was a genius. Terry had been there and done it all in the game – his man-management skills were second to none. We started to slowly climb the league and he started to pull rabbits out of the hat, bringing in players of real quality for peanuts, like Glyn Riley and Alan Walsh. He also turned Keith Curle from a striker to a defender which was a massive surprise to all of us, including Keith, but it worked and he just took off in terms of his career, ending up playing for England.

Although the Fulham game will always be the one that sticks with me, I also have to mention two other games in the red shirt that shows the progression of the club. The first is that memorable night against Hereford United in the semi-final of the Freight Rover Trophy. We appeared to be dead and buried from the first leg at their place after losing 2–0. Terry just told us that we had blown it, and before the second leg he said that he heard the Hereford side had been measured up for their Wembley suits. It was brilliant man-management as it really fired us up. We won 3–0 and, in terms of being ecstatic, nothing will ever beat that night as we felt we had done it for the fans as a way of thanking them when we were rock bottom in the league. It was real turnaround. We were on the brink of extinction and here we were going to a Wembley final, in the days when the only games at that great stadium were England matches, the FA Cup Final and the League Cup Final. I was going to sit in a dressing room that had been used by some of the world's great players. I was truly overcome with emotion that night against Hereford. We went on to win the game at Wembley, which was a real thrill, and went back the following year, unfortunately losing on penalties to Mansfield Town.

When Terry moved upstairs he brought in player-manager Joe Jordan, who again was a fantastic man to play for. Joe again had done it all – he commanded respect wherever he went. I remember one game against Bradford City where he played as a lone striker up front. He absolutely tore the back four apart on his own. Coming off the pitch I will always remember seeing three of the back four of Bradford and I have never seen so much blood on players' shirts in all my life. With Joe in charge he implemented many things that he had learnt from his time in Italy, like different ways of training and diets. This all led to us becoming better players.

In Joe's time, I remember the League Cup semi-final against Nottingham Forest at Ashton Gate. We drew 1–1 at their place and lost 1–0 at home in extra time, and could have won it late on when Walshy unfortunately hit the post. I was so proud of the club, again considering where they had been since I joined them. We had gone toe to toe with one of the best teams in the country at the time and nearly beat them in front of the nation's TV cameras. We felt that we had put a marker down as to what we could achieve in the future.

Unfortunately, Joe left to take over at Hearts in Scotland, and Jimmy Lumsden, his number two, was promoted to manager. I was enjoying a testimonial at the club when out of the blue an offer of £600,000 arrived from Premier League Norwich City. I was flattered but I thought the club would turn it down, but they accepted it, and once your club does that the writing is on the wall. There was a lot of animosity towards me for going from some sections of the fans due to me receiving a testimonial, but if City had turned the offer down there was no way I would have left. In fact, my ultimate goal was to get the club into the Premier League. So I left the Robins and joined the Canaries after playing around 500 games for City.

I enjoyed Norwich. In terms of the club they were like City: same sort of fan base and no real stars, but they did have a really good side with the likes of Chris Sutton, Mark Bowen, Ruel Fox, Jeremy Goss – the list was endless to be honest. With Norwich I enjoyed the Premier League, and when we topped it for a few weeks I remember thinking there can't be many players who have been bottom of the Fourth Division and top of the Premier League in their career. We also had that magical run in the UEFA Cup where we knocked out Bayern Munich, beating them at home, something that no British side has ever done since. We also had two great games in the following round against Inter Milan, who unfortunately knocked us out. Again, during those matches I couldn't help but think about those games for City at the foot of the Fourth Division.

I spent around six years at Carrow Road and got an offer to go to Southend United as a player with a view to being manager David Webb's assistant. I had done all my badges and it was something I couldn't wait to get into. After a year, Dave left and I became manager, which was a really tough job. I kept Southend mid-table which was great, but the fans and the chairman wanted to push on to get success and wanted me to do it by cutting my budget in half, which was almost impossible. In the end I was sacked and ended up at Cambridge United, which again was a case of firefighting but keeping the club competitive, with no money. Again, another almost impossible job to do and after a year I was sacked.

I was then recommended by people in the game to Bournemouth manager Kevin Bond, who was looking for an assistant. We met up and I accepted the offer to work with him. I loved the job as I was still involved in the game and had a real belief in my ability. I kept my playing registration and still turned out for the reserves now and then, even though it was tough at times. Things went well but the game is a results business and after a few defeats Kevin was sacked at Bournemouth and I went with him.

Looking back on my short spell as a manager, I can't really tell you if I was any good at it as I never really had the tools to do the job. I kept the clubs competitive with no resources at all, so I suppose you would have to ask the fans at those clubs what success is to them. Is it winning trophies or just staying afloat, considering there is no investment to improve the squad? Today I think it's incredibly difficult for young managers to get a foot on the ladder and show what they can do. This is why I follow Lee Johnson's progress at Bristol City so closely as I think he is an exceptionally talented young man with a massive future in the game.

I wasn't out of work for long when I got a call from my old Norwich team-mate Mark Bowen, who was Mark Hughes's assistant at Manchester City. He told me that the club had been taken over by Sheikh Mansour, whose family were from Abu Dhabi and worth an apparent £1bn. They had one aim and that was to be the best at everything: best ground, best team, best youngsters, best club, and would I be interested in working as one of the recruitment scouts. I didn't take long to give him an answer. In the early days I was in charge of looking after games in Spain, which I did for two years, going every weekend to watch games in La Liga, and before that I was assigned to Italy. That was over ten years ago.

Today I am in charge of international recruitment at the club. We have various scouts assigned to countries all over Europe. Each scout will watch all the games in their assigned country. The philosophy is based on the fact that before, the club were agent-led and there were many bridges burned between UK clubs and clubs abroad due to the way transfers were done. We have decided that this practice will not carry on and we have to repair those bridges. Sheikh is very much about transparency, honesty and a bond of a handshake, which means that each scout will speak to all the clubs in their particular league and build relationships with them. They also tell them that Manchester City may well get linked with their players but if they have not heard directly from the scout then the reports are not true. This cuts out agents trying to engineer moves for players at inflated prices. The other side of the coin is that the club know of every player in those leagues, and if another club signs them it's not because we missed them, but due to them not being good enough for us or we won't pay the money. It is proving successful and it shows how important the role of recruitment is in today's game.

I can't say I haven't been given the tools by Manchester City, which are what you need at any level of the game to be successful. It's ironic when I think about how my career started and the amount of money that is awash in the game today. People like Terry Cooper and those players who tore up their contracts made me the player I was. They gave me lessons in life that I could not have got anywhere else. My time at Bristol City will always be my favourite time in football. We were young lads starting out and every side I played in had an incredible team spirit which came from the managers we had. I will always see it as a privilege to have worn the red shirt of City and to have been at the start of that great club's rise from the depths of the leagues.

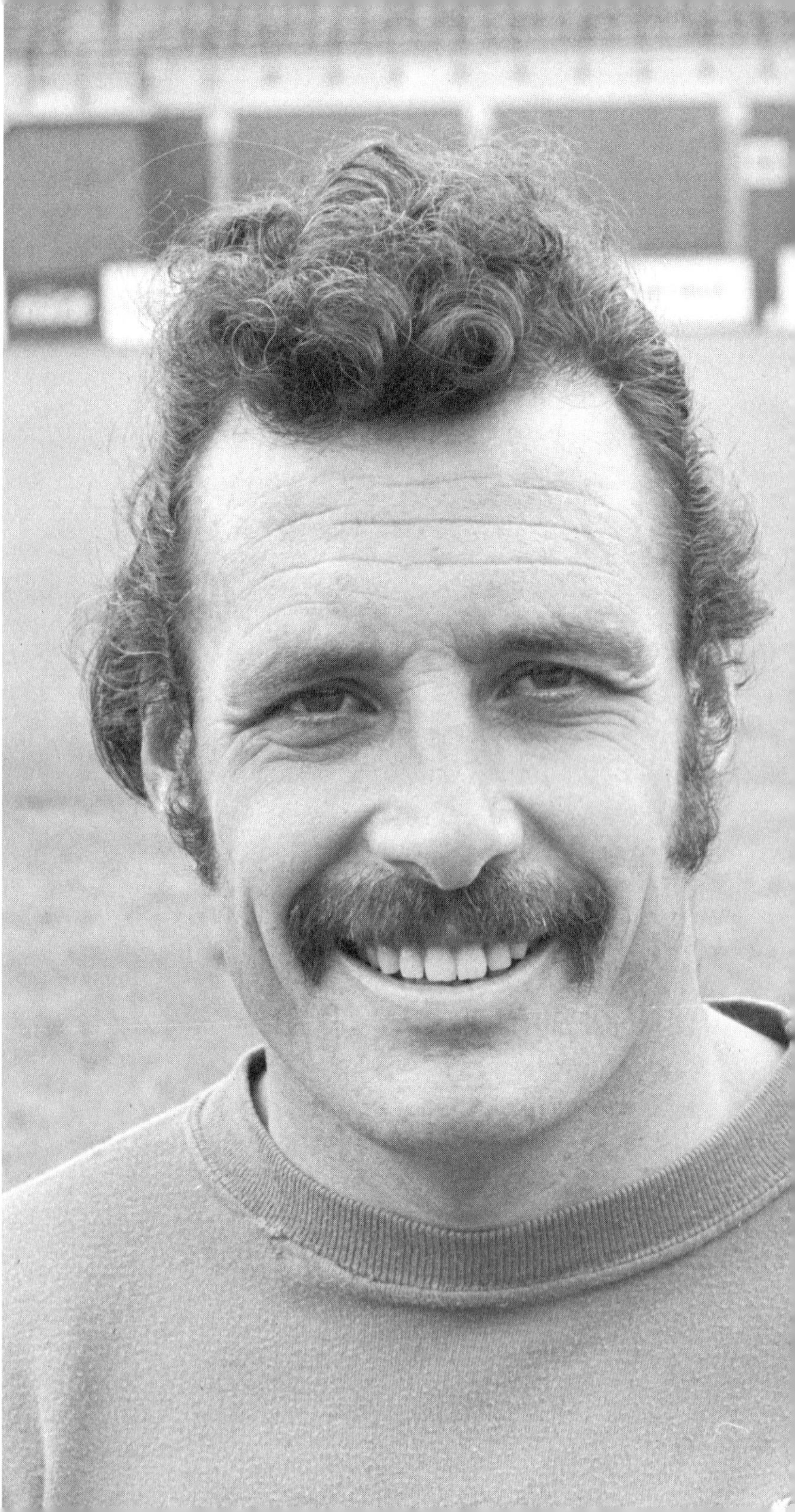

GORDON PARR

Gordon Parr

In Gordon Parr, Bristol City had a defender who never gave up, both on and off the field. The wing-half-cum-defender was noted for his power and pace rather than the finer points of the game, although it took this former Bristol Boys captain a few years to show the City fans what he could do. Gordon made his debut for the Robins, as a 19-year-old, in 1957 but never really became a regular until the late sixties. In today's game Gordon would probably have been released by City or he would have asked for a move to find first-team football somewhere else, but as far as he was concerned he wanted to battle away to get in the first team. Eventually he became the backbone of manager Fred Ford's team, building a formidable partnership at the back with Jack Connor. After 15 years' loyalty and service at the club Gordon was let go by manager Alan Dicks who had plans for the emerging Geoff Merrick to take Gordon's place in the side. Gordon left the club, so Bristol City, as a fitting send-off, organised a successful testimonial against Chelsea. Parr eventually signed for Waterford in the Irish League where he won a title and played in the European Cup. Gordon returned to the south-west after a season and played non-league for Minehead.

Bristol City 4 Ipswich Town 1
Football League Division Two
10 May 1966
Ashton Gate

Bristol City: Gibson, Ford, Briggs, Parr, Connor, Low, Derrick, Bush, Atyeo, Clark, Bartley.

Goals: Bush, Parr, Atyeo 2.

I couldn't believe it when I was asked to take part in this book. Don't get me wrong, I am extremely flattered to be involved, but I would have thought there were so many other players from my time at City who could have been asked. Looking back, I was really in and out of the side for ages and I was certainly not one of the gifted players at the club. I think everyone who saw me play would know that my game really was to win the ball and give it to somebody who could make something happen. I was more of a carrier than the sort of player who could turn a game round.

I was a Knowle West lad who was pursued by Bristol City and Wolverhampton Wanderers. I had captained the Bristol Boys team and that was always an indication that one of the Bristol clubs would be keeping tabs on you. Thankfully for me it was City, as they were my side of the city. I was offered an apprenticeship by City but my dad was not too keen as he said I had to get an apprenticeship before I had any thoughts of playing football for a living. How times have changed. We didn't really have any idea of how to get an apprenticeship but then City chairman Harry Dolman stepped in and offered me one as an electrician with one of his companies. Dad was thrilled and so was Harry as it meant I would also sign for City. I, on the other hand, was just dreaming of being a footballer and pulling on the red shirt. I really had no interest in becoming an electrician, especially as it could take me the best part of six years to qualify.

Combining the two was really hard work, as I would work all week and at nights go training with City, and at weekends play and train with City, but I knew it had to be done. I wasn't one of the standout lads at the time so I knew hard work and perseverance would be the things that might get me into the first team. The manager at the time was Pat Beasley. Pat had played for City and also with Arsenal and Huddersfield Town. He was a decent bloke and the City job was his first appointment. As I said previous, I was never a star in the side, and to be honest I was a bit borderline in terms of getting a crack at the first team, but fair play to Pat, he gave me my debut, which was at home to Middlesbrough in a 0–0 draw.

I was 19 years of age and it's quite funny really when you think of today's players, but I walked to the game from my house in Knowle West along with the supporters. I remember being really nervous and excited during the game, as I was desperate to get on. City at the time had gone six games without a win and were leaking goals for fun. In the second half of the game Alan Williams got injured and Pat sent me on as left-half for about 20 minutes. I got a great reception from the fans as they knew I was a local boy and that was always a bit special for them. I did okay, typical Gordon Parr, nothing fancy, and the draw brought the losing streak to an end. I was picked for two more games that season but then got nowhere near the first team for about three or four seasons and I just became a regular in the reserves.

Pat had left the club in 1958 so things never really changed with Peter Doherty in charge; again I was just in the reserves. It started to get to me but I just had this burning ambition to be a regular at the club. I knew I could have always asked for a move but, the trouble was, I just loved it living in Bristol and I felt that if I left it would be almost like giving up. Peter Doherty came and went and he was replaced by Fred Ford. I liked Fred as he was a real taskmaster, particularly on the training ground where due to my fitness I excelled. I remember running around Ashton Park once with the lads in training and I was out at the front setting the pace and a few of the lads asked me to ease up a bit and Fred heard it. He stopped the training and told us that I was going to run as hard as I could and I wasn't to listen to the rest of the slackers behind me – it was typical Fred.

Again I was in and out of the side and I really became frustrated at not getting a chance. I even had a set-to with Fred once in a tea room at the club after I was left out again. We squared up to each other before we were pulled apart by players and staff. After that I think Fred saw a different side to me, but I was still not a regular. But he did give me a run in the side at right-half the season after where I made about 30 appearances in a City side that would finish third in the league behind eventual winners Carlisle United. It was great to get promotion and I really felt that I had helped, but it was tinged with sadness that I wasn't in the side that beat

Oldham to actually clinch promotion, especially as it was at Ashton Gate in front of our fans. I was there celebrating but it's not the same when you have a club blazer on instead of a kit.

But now we come to my 'Match of my Life', and I could not have asked for a more memorable game to have been part of and that was the home game with Ipswich Town in 1966. It was a game I scored in but, more importantly, it was the great John Atyeo's last game in a Bristol City shirt, and I will be forever privileged to have been part of it. John truly was a gentleman on and off the pitch. He was always available for a chat and always encouraged you if, like me, you were in and out of the side. I had some very memorable chats with him regarding my career at City and I always thought he would have made a great manager one day as he commanded so much respect from everyone. It was a momentous evening and an incredibly emotional night for fans, players and all the backroom staff. I felt a bit sorry for the Ipswich lads as they knew they were going to be in the middle of a mass celebration of Bristol City's greatest player.

The Ipswich game was the last of the season and the backbone of the side that season were Mike Gibson, Tony Ford, Alec Briggs, Jack Connor, Gordon Low, Roger Peters, John Atyeo and Brian Clark, with myself, Jantzen Derrick, Gerry Sharpe and Terry Bush doing our bit. We had a decent season, losing only eight games, which was only bettered by champions Manchester

City, but our downfall was that we drew too many games. If we had turned those draws into wins we could have been looking at another promotion. Instead we finished fifth in the league, three points off promotion. The atmosphere at Ashton Gate was incredible and the pressure on John was just as intense. It was his 645th appearance for the club and it was a career that had spanned about 15 years with City and England. In that time he had scored 348 goals for the club. Irrespective of the result, the night belonged to John, but we all wanted him to go out with a win.

There was a massive build-up to the game in the local papers. It seemed as though everyone was talking about it. John gave a speech to us all in the dressing room before the game and he thanked us all for our efforts this season. Then Fred Ford spoke along with chairman Harry Dolman, who pointed out how special John was. We all clapped and the whole place was buzzing. John stayed in the changing room as we left and we all shook his hand as we went to the tunnel along with Ipswich, and we all filed out on to the pitch side by side. Along with us were some of the City team that he had made his debut with some 15 years ago: Cyril Williams, Jack Boxley, Alec Eisentrager, Ernie Peacock, Pat Beasley, Fred Stone, Dennis Roberts and Jack Bailey. John then came out of the tunnel on his own to a hero's welcome. We then posed for a photo and got in our positions for the game. The ref blew his whistle and Ashton Gate roared as we kicked off.

It was a tense affair as we were a bit nervous for John more than anything. Then with ten minutes on the clock, Ipswich spoiled the party when their forward Crawford stuck the ball home from close range. The atmosphere went dead as we desperately tried to get an equaliser. We pushed forward and Crawford nearly got another five minutes later, but some great goalkeeping from Mike Gibson kept him out. Minutes later we got our chance when Terry Bush slammed the ball home and the party started up again. The crowd got louder and louder but we just couldn't make a breakthrough. I remember some sections of them booing us off at half-time as they were so disappointed for John. Fred Ford told us to keep going second half and chances would come. John also told us we had to stick at it.

The second half was just as tough. They had a few close efforts and so did we. The crowd were starting to get restless when all of a sudden we were awarded a throw-in. I started to run forward and Brian Clark took it quickly. It fell perfectly for me in acres of space. I could see their keeper coming out so I lobbed the ball over him and into the net. It was incredible; the fans went wild and so did we. It felt so wonderful to have scored on John's big day – I will never forget it. With that, Ipswich seemed to have had their lot. We piled on the pressure and the fans were willing for John to get on the scoresheet. We got a corner with 15 minutes to go, and Ashton Gate ramped up the noise. Bartley put in an inswinger and John rose to flick it into the net off his head. I have never heard a noise like it; everyone was going crazy. When things settled down we got at them again and I got a chance late on just at the edge of the box. I swivelled to create some space, then had a shot that was blocked by the keeper. Then in ran John like an 18-year-old to slam the ball home and get his 350th goal. The rest is history. Crowds poured on – it was bedlam. Poor old Ipswich were in the middle of a party they could not get out of, and when the whistle went there were tears from everyone – players, staff and supporters. It was the greatest day in my Bristol City career.

It really was a game that, looking back, I am extremely honoured to have been part of. It's become part of the history of this great club over the years and I will never forget it or the great John Atyeo. Another game that springs to mind was in the FA Cup against Tottenham Hotspur the following year. I was marking Jimmy Greaves and I did really well, except that I took my eye off Jimmy in the first half and he scored. He then went on to score a penalty in the second half making it 2–0. We also had a League Cup disappointment against the men from North London in 1970, when we were beaten in a two-legged semi-final. I remember the defeat really hurt as we were so close to getting to Wembley for the first time.

Fred Ford left the club in the 1967/68 season and he was replaced by Alan Dicks. Alan was a young manager and was starting to build a new side based on a lot of the youngsters that were coming through. For me, I was competing with a local lad who would go on to be one of the club's legends: Geoff Merrick. Geoff was a great lad who was always willing to learn and he was a born leader. Dicks was totally upfront that I was not really in his plans and in 1972 I played my last game for the club in a 2–2 draw away at Norwich City. At the time I didn't know it would be my last, but I knew the writing was on the wall. I left the club as I knew I wasn't going to be playing, plus this time I never had the luxury of time on my side. Fair play to the club, they granted me a testimonial game, which was organised by Chris Garland, who had just gone to Chelsea. Chris brought the Londoners down and it was a packed house for my send-off, which was really touching for myself and my family.

I had a few offers on the table. One in particular intrigued me and it was from the former Manchester United full-back Shay Brennan, who had become manager of Waterford Football Club over in Ireland. Shay convinced me to sign for a year. The club would pay for me to travel over on Saturdays, play the games on Sundays and come back to Bristol on the Mondays. I agreed and over I went. The standard wasn't brilliant but if I'm honest it suited me as I wasn't getting any younger. The supporters were great and we won the Irish League which meant we qualified for the European Cup. Unfortunately we were knocked out early on by AC Omonia of Cyprus 3–2 over two legs, but it was a fantastic experience, especially as it was happening so late in my career. I only stayed about 18 months which was longer than I had planned; I knew it wasn't going to be a long-term arrangement. I left and came back to Bristol where I signed for non-league Minehead and stayed two years before I hung up my boots and went back to being an electrician.

I have loved thinking about my time at City and it always touches me when I go back to watch a game or go to a function and fans come up to me. I was never the 'golden boy' at the club and many felt I should have moved on, but I just wanted to play for Bristol City and nobody else, which I don't think was a bad thing.

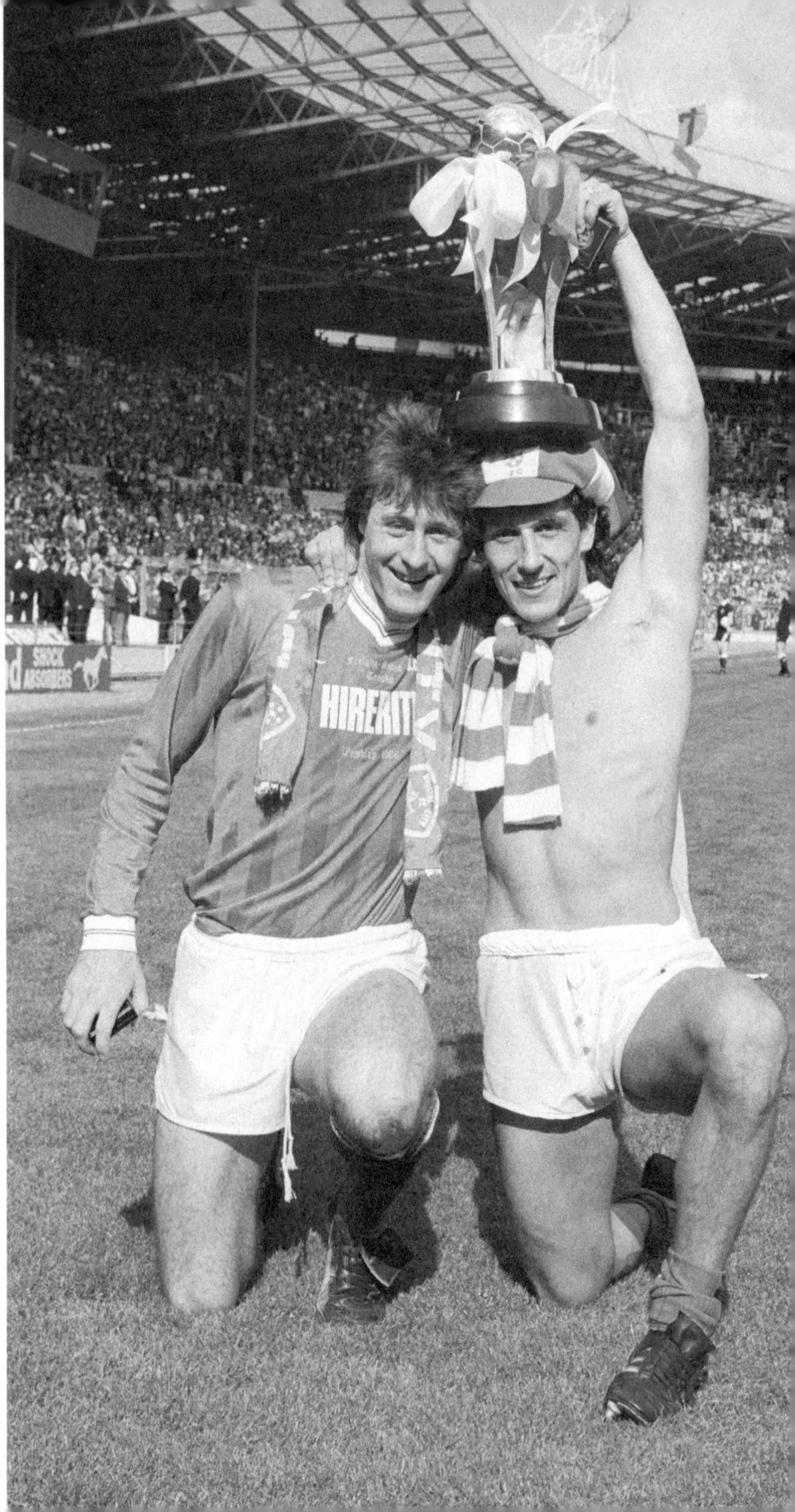

GLYN RILEY

Glyn Riley

When Glyn Riley arrived at Bristol City from Barnsley in 1982, City were at their lowest, on and off the field. The club had just avoided extinction and found themselves in the Fourth Division. Yet this charismatic striker from Yorkshire lifted the club on the field with his battling, no-nonsense displays for manager Terry Cooper's young side. And with his exuberant personality he brought a buzz about the place that had been lacking for years. Riley had skill and strength in abundance. He topped the club's goals chart in his first two seasons at Ashton Gate. His positivity around team-mates helped to rebuild the club and gave them the optimism to go forward and achieve promotion in the 1983/84 season. But it was his performance and two goals in City's Freight Rover Final win at Wembley two years later against Bolton Wanderers that secured him in the history of the club forever. Always a fans' favourite, Riley would go on and spend four years at the club before moving to Aldershot and subsequent retirement. When supporters talk about greats from different eras, Glyn is surely at the very top of 1980s heroes.

Bristol City 3 Bolton Wanderers 0
Freight Rover Final
24 May 1986
Wembley Stadium

Bristol City: Waugh, Newman, Williams, Curle, Moyes, Riley, Pritchard, Hutchinson, Harle, Walsh, Neville. Sub: Llewellyn.

Goals: Riley 2, Pritchard.

It's really enjoyable for me to talk about the 'Match of my Life' with Bristol City Football Club. I have had some great times at the club and, looking back, it really was the best time of my career. There really is only one match, though, that will stay with me forever and that's the Freight Rover Final against Bolton Wanderers in 1986, in which I scored two goals. To be able to say I scored two goals in a Wembley final is the stuff of dreams and the whole experience will be remembered by me forever. It's really touching also to meet up with the team and supporters now and again and see how much that day meant to every one of them.

The competition was really in its infancy and I remember telling the local paper that the crowd will probably be one man and his dog for some of the games. I got into hot water with Bristol City manager Terry Cooper for saying it to a journalist, but in the early rounds I was proved right. We played Plymouth Argyle and Walsall and beat them both so the momentum within the team was building, as was the interest from supporters as the crowds started to grow. Our league form was a bit inconsistent but from a personal point of view I was finding the net along with my striking partner Steve Neville.

The competition really started to take momentum when we drew Gillingham in the area semi-final and there were about 6,000 at Gillingham that night, which for a midweek night game wasn't that bad. We beat the Gills and found ourselves in an area final against

Hereford United over two legs with the winners going to Wembley for the final. There was a good crowd at Hereford and we really fancied our chances against them. Unfortunately we were terrible on the night and were well beaten 2–0. As we walked off the pitch I think I knew deep down that it was going to take a massive effort to turn this around. In the dressing room after, manager Terry Cooper just said, 'You have just blown your chance to get to Wembley.' He then just slammed the door and left. We all looked at each other and we felt he was right.

The second leg was really pumped up by the local press. Even though we were 2–0 down from the first leg, Bristol City had never been to Wembley and this was going to be their greatest chance to get there. As players, we had got rid of the heartache of the first leg and we were so determined to turn things around. We were up for it and no real team talk was needed. Ashton Gate was incredible. The supporters never stopped singing and we got the result we needed, beating them 3–0. At the final whistle the whole of the crowd came on to the pitch and I eventually got to the dressing room in just my shorts and socks as the rest of my kit was taken off me by fans. The celebrations were fantastic with everybody dreaming of Wembley.

We found out that we would be playing against Bolton Wanderers who we had a very good record against that season, so we again were very confident. The build-up to the final was twice as much as the build-up to the semi-final. You have to remember back then the only games at Wembley were the FA Cup Final, the League Cup Final and various England internationals, so for supporters and players of lower clubs like we were, this was the stuff of dreams. There was the usual buzz of trying to get tickets for family and friends, and on the local TV there was always a story about queues at Ashton Gate as people got their tickets. Every coach company in Bristol was fully booked taking supporters along the M4 to the game. We got measured for our Wembley suits and the whole build-up was like a dream. As for Terry Cooper, he trained us like dogs for the two weeks leading up to the game. He ran us all over Ashton Gate, up and down the stands; it was like a preseason. He kept telling us he wanted us to be ready, and we were.

We went up a couple of days before and stayed in the Vandervault Hotel in London. We trained, then we went to the stadium and trained on the pitch and it was like a lovely lush carpet. No disrespect, but it was nothing like any pitch we had played on during the league campaign. We walked round the stadium. I remember the baths were all individual and massive and we looked up to the Royal Box wondering if we would be going up as winners or losers the following day. When matchday arrived we drove to the stadium and it was a sea of red and white. I think City took around 50,000 fans for the game, so along with Bolton, it was pretty much a full house, which was incredible. Terry didn't say too much to us; he just told us to enjoy it and remember it. I felt really confident as I was finding the net easily that season and I just knew I needed a chance. Bolton Wanderers had some experienced players in their squad, like Asa Hartford, Phil Neal and Sam Allardyce, so they were certainly not going to roll over.

When we walked out, the sound was deafening. The weather was boiling hot and I remember looking ahead and just seeing all the Bolton fans singing and cheering, but as I turned round the City fans, who were in the tunnel end, erupted and it brought me out in goosebumps. 'City, City, City' just seemed to ring around the ground. From the kick-off they battered us and we just couldn't get going. I remember after the game Terry telling me that for the first 15 minutes he thought he had trained us too hard in the build-up. They had a great chance from an Asa Hartford corner that bounced against the bar. We eventually weathered the storm and started to get into the match and have some chances. Rob Newman got a chance and his header just glanced the post. Then I had my back to goal with a defender behind me; I span round and just curled a shot the wrong side of the post which gave me such a lift. It was all us now and I think our early nerves had gone. Then on 44 minutes Keith Curle put a ball into the box which Bobby Hutchinson went up for with their keeper, and it fell just right for me so I struck it. The ball seemed to go towards the net in slow motion as we all watched it, and when it crashed into the net the City fans went wild and I just ran to them. It was a moment that gets me emotional even to this day when I recall it. As I ran, I thought about the young kid from Barnsley who played with his mates, all dreaming of scoring a goal in a Wembley cup final, and here I was doing it. The team eventually caught up with me and we went back to the centre spot with 'City, City, City' ringing around the ground.

Terry said to us at half-time, 'You have done what was needed, now go and finish them off.' We ran out supremely confident in the second half. I got another chance but the ball just sat too high for me and I stuck it over the bar. If it had been on a Football League pitch I would have scored but the Wembley pitch was like a sponge and the ball sprung up too high; that's my excuse anyway. We got our second after the keeper fumbled and it fell for Howard Pritchard and he just crashed it in. We knew then that Bolton were finished. Asa Hartford, who was stunning in the opening 20 minutes, was now more preoccupied with trying to kick Keith Curle than anything else. Me and Steve Neville were pulling their back two all over the park, which was creating so many chances for us. Then six minutes from time we had a great move which culminated in a great cross that landed on my head perfectly for me to steer into the net. Off I ran and jumped over the hoardings and on to my backside.

Unfortunately I felt a massive pain go down my legs, which was cramp. I asked a ball boy to stretch my legs, which he did. All the lads were now all over me and, as we ran back to the centre circle, I could see a man in a white coat stood up on the scoreboard changing the score with a three and also spelling out the name RILEY. It brought a lump to my throat as I thought of Geoff Hurst in the World Cup, and here I was, a lad from Barnsley, with my name on the Wembley scoreboard. In no time the whistle went and we had won. We just hugged everyone.

It was a massive thing for Terry and the club as four years earlier they had almost gone into liquidation, and here they were being cheered on by 50,000 City fans in a Wembley cup final. We climbed the steps to get the cup and I could see my wife and people from the club. I never really wanted to leave the pitch as we ran round with the trophy. That evening I was late down for the dinner in the hotel and when I did arrive the cup was placed on my seat. It was an incredible weekend with a tour of Bristol days later and dinner with the Lord Mayor. I remember going back the following year in the competition against Mansfield Town. I scored again but we drew 1–1 and lost 5–4 in a penalty shoot-out. I was gutted, so I did get to experience both emotions in a Wembley final.

I had some great times at Bristol City and it really was, I think, the pinnacle of my career. I started as a youngster at Barnsley and was given my debut by manager Jim Iley aged 16 and 142 days, again another game I remember. Jim brought me on as a sub with 20 minutes to go. With my first touch, the full-back hit me right into the advertising hoardings, then I scored with about ten minutes to go. It was a real baptism of fire as the opposing defenders really got stuck into me, but you just got on with it back then. I learnt so much back in those days. We played Sheffield Wednesday in front of 38,000 at Hillsborough and I was playing up front with Allan Clark. We both scored. I was about 18 and Allan was in his thirties and he talked me through the whole game.

Norman Hunter came to the club and he had so much knowledge of the game. But it was Norman who eventually let me go. I had a few injuries and I was in and out of the side. Norman told me I would be a squad player and he would let me go on a free transfer, which would mean it would be easier for me to find a club. Terry Cooper had seen me and was interested, along with Huddersfield Town. I came down to Bristol with my wife and met Terry. He showed us around different places to live and really sold the club to me and I signed. I arrived with Alan Crawford, who City had got from Chesterfield. They also got John Shaw and Tom Ritchie to return to the club and the rest of the side were young kids. I had my debut at home to Hull City and I scored in a 2–1 win, which really helped with supporters and created a bond that has never gone away.

In total I was at City for about four years and scored 77 goals in 231 games. I eventually left through, again, injuries which meant me not being a regular in the side. There was interest from Swindon Town, but I eventually decided on Aldershot Town. I was there under Lennie Lawrence for 18 months and played twice against City. The reception the fans gave me on my return to Ashton Gate was incredible; it was great to be remembered by them. After my 18 months I realised it was time to hang up the boots and go into the business world, which I did. I also played for Bath City along with old City team-mate Rob Newman for a while and scored a 35-yard screamer against Dorchester Town, which proved to be my last goal in football. Today I am involved in business and travel the world skiing with my wife. I go to City now and again for various hospitality days and reunions and it's great to see what those two goals meant to fans, as they meant everything to me.

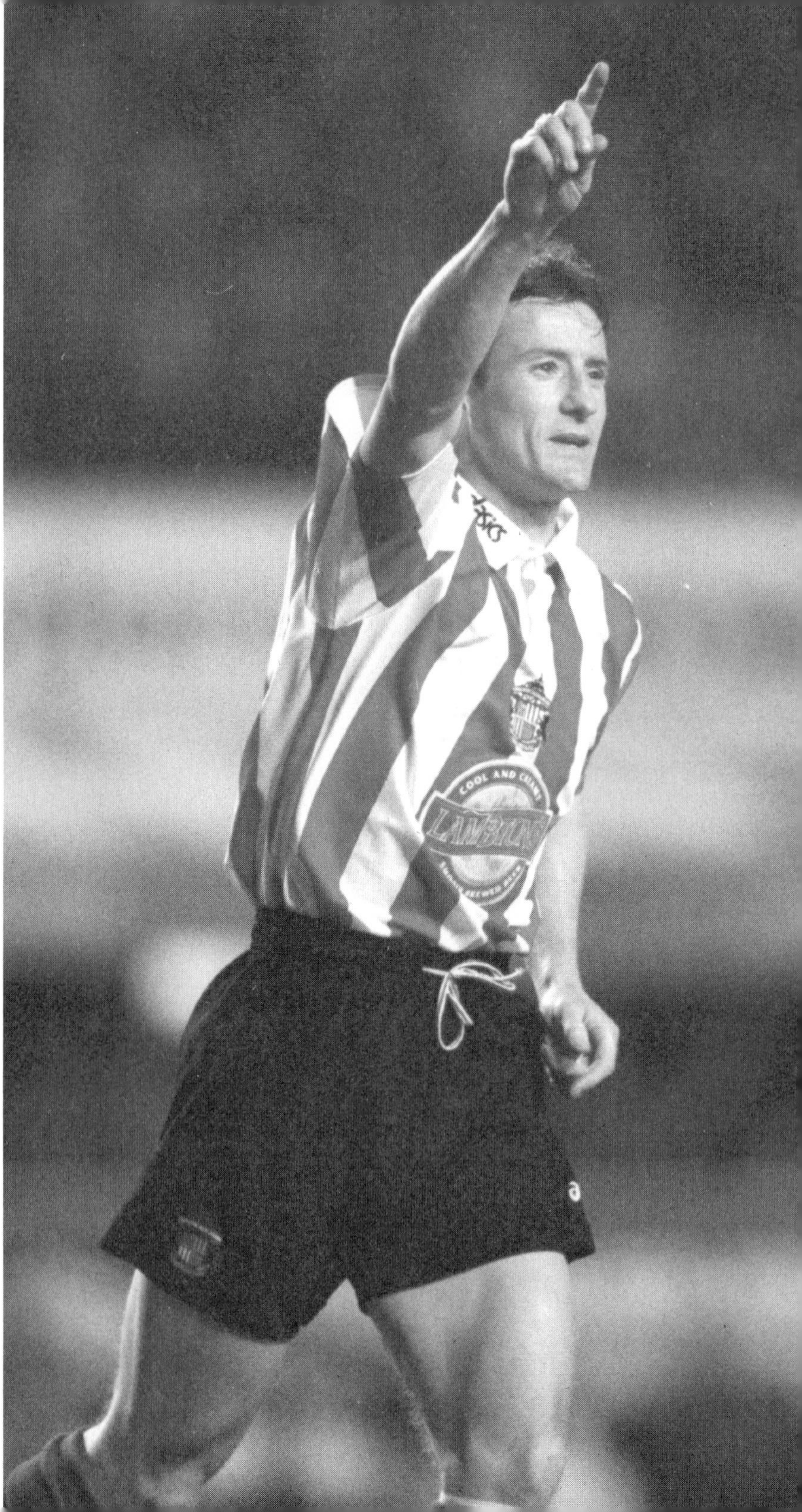

MARTIN SCOTT

Martin Scott

Yorkshire man Martin Scott arrived at Ashton Gate in 1990 and had the respect and admiration of not only supporters but also fellow team-mates from day one. This versatile, pacey full-back made his name at Rotherham United where he found first-team football as a 16-year-old and came to the attention of a host of clubs and in particular Bristol City, who eventually paid £200,000 for his services, money that saved Rotherham at the time from possible administration. Scott became Mr Dependable at Ashton Gate. As managers came and went, his 100 per cent attitude on the field became a huge hit with the supporters. Scott's impeccable displays for City again brought attention from various clubs, but eventually a £750,000 bid from Sunderland became too much for the club's board to turn down. So City's prized asset at the time left for Roker Park. Not surprisingly he became an instant hit with the Roker fans. With Sunderland, Scott graced the Premiership before a dreadful injury meant him hanging up his boots. A successful spell in coaching and management at Hartlepool United followed, before he stepped out of football and started his own successful coaching academy throughout the north-east.

Bristol City 1 Sheffield Wednesday 1
Football League Division Two
8 December 1990
Ashton Gate

Bristol City: Sinclair, Llewellyn, Newman, Rennie, Scott, Bent, Shelton, May, Smith, Taylor, Morgan. Subs: Bryant, Allison.

Goal: Shirtliff (own goal).

I really do have a very strong love for this football club. When I played here I think it was probably the best football of my career. In fact, I have nothing but affection for the club and I get a real sense of love and respect from the supporters whenever I come back for games or any sort of function. This was really evident at the start of the year when I was asked to attend the 25th anniversary of us beating Liverpool at Anfield in the FA Cup. I agreed straightaway and flew down for the event which was organised by the Bristol City Supporters Club. The night was fantastic and I met so many of the old team from that special night at Anfield. The real buzz, though, was seeing the supporters and getting a great response from them, as well as seeing people who worked at the club back then, like ground staff and secretaries – they were all wonderful.

So when I was asked to contribute to the 'Match of my Life' book I knew there would be so many games to choose from that I would be a bit stuck for choice. After all, there were those great games against Liverpool and some great nights against rivals Rovers, plus a few cup games here and there. But I thought long and hard and, although the Liverpool games I will never forget, as I played against some of the country's great players and did well, the one game will always be my debut for Bristol City, and this is how I got there.

I was born in Sheffield and I used to watch both United and Wednesday with my dad. Football wasn't on the TV as much then as it is today so I was just dying to see any sort of football I could. Rotherham showed interest in me at the age of 12, but although I was a focused kid I was small and a real late developer. At 14 I was offered a Youth Training Scheme with the club, which I took up, but I really had to work on the physicality of my game as, due to my size, many thought I wouldn't make the grade. At 16 I went from 5ft 2in to 5ft 10in and found myself in the Rotherham first team. Looking back, I don't think teams would have stuck with me like Rotherham did. The growing I did caused me a problem with my pelvis which meant I needed an operation which kept me out for a summer, so I was always loyal to Rotherham as they stuck with me through those times and there was never ever any suggestion that I would be released.

My debut was away at York City where we lost 1–0. I was naive and raw but gave 100 per cent and I remember manager Norman Hunter telling me '100% lad, that's all you have to give'. I loved my time at Rotherham and they were a side that always taught me good habits. I was so proud when we won the Third Division title in my first year there. But I always wanted to improve and test myself against a higher level, so when Bristol City came in for me I couldn't really say no. As far as Rotherham United were concerned, they couldn't say no either, as the £200,000 City had offered was a lifeline for them at the time. I was thinking of leaving the year before when my contract had run out but I signed a new one so Rotherham would get something for me when I did eventually leave.

Bristol was a massive step up for me and I knew a bit about the city and the club. It was very much like Sheffield in terms of size and it also had two sides, so I knew there was rivalry across the city. It was Jimmy Lumsden who signed me and I'm sure I was his first signing at the club. The dressing room I came into was experienced but with not much youth in there. I knew Gary Shelton from his exploits at Sheffield Wednesday and I knew Mark Aizlewood, who was at Leeds United.

And so to my debut for the Robins which funnily enough was against Sheffield Wednesday. Wednesday were a real multimillion-pound side at the time and in the top three of the division. They had a high-profile manager in Ron Atkinson and players of the calibre of Trevor Francis, David Hirst, John Sheridan and Carlton Palmer, so they were certainly no pushovers. As far as I was concerned I would be picking up Trevor Francis, who was the game's first million-pound player back in the day and a fantastic player for England over many years – so no pressure then, on my debut. I didn't really have time to get together with the City lads but they were fantastic to me. My mum and dad were coming down from Sheffield for the game but they broke down on the way due to the snow. I think they eventually just made it in time for kick-off.

The conditions were terrible: the snow was driving down on us through the whole game. I had a steady start and got a few good tackles in, which seemed to please the fans. I remember Jimmy telling me one of the criticisms of the team in the past was that they didn't get stuck in as much as they should have in games. Wednesday went close in the first couple of minutes when David Hirst, who was a real handful, clipped the post with a header. Then full-back Andy Llewellyn lost possession to Trevor Francis and his cross-field ball fell perfect for Danny Wilson to sweep the ball home and put them 1–0 up. We regrouped and, in minutes, City midfielder Andy May chipped a ball over the top of the defence for Dave Smith to run on to and Wednesday's defender Shirtliff put the ball into his own net. It was quite a start and the crowd were brilliant – I remember they cheered every tackle I put in.

The second half to be honest belonged to Wednesday. They put us under the cosh and had a few chances to finish us off. I remember clearing the ball off the City line after another Wednesday attack. The game finished 1–1 and I got a tremendous reaction from the City fans. I knew then that this was the club for me. After the game I was voted man of the match by the Supporters Club which was a great honour. I left the ground clutching my man of the match bottle of whisky, which seemed appropriate given the weather conditions, and I was told that my mum and dad along with me and the wife could not travel back to Sheffield as we were snowed in. This also applied to the Wednesday team who had to make it back to their hotel in Bristol. As for me and the family, we were put up for the night by City chairman Des Williams and his wife at their house. That gesture showed my family what a great club it was and how I was going to be happy there. The game will always be important to me as it was my first taste of the fans and theirs of me, and it seemed to start a great relationship that carried on throughout my City career.

I also loved the games against rivals Bristol Rovers. I never realised there was such a rivalry in the city between the two clubs, but the atmosphere created at those games was truly unforgettable and a real experience to play in. They were games you knew meant so much to the supporters, and if I'm honest it meant so much to both sets of players as well. It's a shame they don't happen that often due to them now being in different leagues – they were certainly torrid, intense games.

My career at City went from strength to strength. I won the Supporters Club player of the year in 1991/92, which still means a lot to me, and my family were really happy in the city. Obviously I will mention the games against Liverpool when we had our cup run. They were brilliant games to have been involved in, especially for myself and Andy Llewellyn, as we were up against players of the quality of John Barnes, Steve McManaman and Mark Walters, who were all brilliant wingers at the top of their game. So to go one to one with them and come off the better was brilliant for us, and I think the whole team came to the attention of a lot of clubs due to our display over the three games with them. That was the most pleasing thing for all of us – that this result at Anfield was no fluke. We deserved it over the games we had played with them and I think that's why the Kop responded by giving us a standing ovation at the end of the game. It was probably my proudest memory in football coming off that pitch at Anfield, and I know what it still means to the fans as they were incredible with their memories about the event at the recent 25-year anniversary at Ashton Gate. It's why I made the effort to come down for it.

I had played under a few managers at City. Jimmy Lumsden signed me, and in my time at the club Jimmy had been replaced by Denis Smith, then Russell Osman became player-manager then boss. It was Russell after all who, along with his assistant Tony Fawthrop, masterminded the Liverpool defeat, but as is the way with football Russell was replaced and Joe Jordan, who had come back to the club for a second time, was given the manager's job. I probably didn't get on great at first with Joe but I see him now and since I became a manager I understand a bit more of how my move away from the club came about. Joe was obviously told by the board that he had to generate his own money if he wanted to bring players in, so I was one of the club's main assets.

So it's December 1994 and my family are getting ready for Christmas where we are going to have keeper Keith Welch and his family round. I am at training and I get a call to come to Ashton Gate immediately. I jump in the car and arrive at the car park only to be met by

Joe Jordan with a black plastic bag with my boots and the contents of my locker in it. Joe says, 'Martin, here's your things. The club have sold you to Sunderland. They want you to go up tonight to agree terms'. Obviously I was shocked and said 'Well, I will speak to them to see if it's okay and go tomorrow.' Joe replied, 'I don't think you understand. The club have sold you; you have to go tonight and sign.' So I phoned my wife, who was working at House of Fraser in Bristol, and told her the news. She was as shell-shocked as I was. It was two days before Christmas and we had all this upheaval. We both got in the car and drove to Yorkshire where we met Sunderland manager Mick Buxton in a hotel. It was then I found out that the fee was £750,000 plus player Gary Owers coming the other way. I talked with Mick and we were literally about £10,000 apart in terms of wages. I explained that this was a big move for me. Mick understood and went away to make a phone call. In the meantime Joe rang me and asked what the stumbling block was. After telling him, he said leave it with him and within minutes Mick came back and said they had agreed to my terms. We stayed in the hotel and drove up to Sunderland the following day.

I laugh now when I speak to Joe about the move and he says it was handled terribly, but he was desperate for me to sign so he could get some money in. At the time I phoned ex-City boss Denis Smith who had managed Sunderland and I asked him what the club was like. He told me, 'Sign for them; they will love you and you will love them; you are their sort of player,' which was nice to hear. Sunderland were in the same league as City but just above them, but you could see they were a club going places with a new stadium on the horizon. It took me months to settle, though, as there was a lot of pressure on me. The club had just sold striker Don Goodman to Wolves for a million and the fans wanted another striker, but they forked out £750,000 for a left-back which a lot of the fans couldn't understand.

With all this going on, my wife and I didn't get back to Bristol until January 14th, and we had to throw out all our Christmas food that was still in the fridge, and also sell our house in Nailsea, just outside Bristol. We were in a hotel in Sunderland for three months before we bought a property up there. I struggled in the north-east to start with and unfortunately so did the team as results didn't go our way. Manager Mick Buxton lost his job with six games to go till the end of the season with us perilously close to the drop. The club brought in Peter Reid who was a revelation in keeping us up. Unfortunately Bristol City went down. I really felt for the lads back in Bristol as they were a great bunch.

My game flourished under Reid and he took us all the way to the Premiership, which was just fantastic to play in. That first season under Reid cemented my relationship with the fans as they could see what I could do now I was happier. I loved playing in the Premiership against the game's best and in front of full houses. I kept thinking of that lad at Rotherham United who many felt was too small to play. Unfortunately injury was just round the corner. We went to Lincoln City in the FA Cup and it was a horrible night on a real bobbly pitch. We won 1–0 but I went up for a ball and fell awkwardly and knew something was not right. I had broken my leg and snapped all the ankle ligaments, so it was like two bad injuries in one. I was out for a year and also spent 13 weeks at Lilleshall rehabilitation centre away from the family. In that time I was offered a further two-year deal as my contract had run out.

I got back but the leg still wasn't right. Then I got called to Peter Reid's office and he told me the offer had been withdrawn on medical advice. So here I was, 30 years of age, and now a free agent. Ipswich Town were keen on taking me, but then Paul Jewell at Bradford City called. Bradford had just been promoted to the Premiership and two years before he had a bid of one million turned down by Sunderland, so he was overjoyed to get me for free. He offered me a three-year deal, which I accepted. I played preseason but broke down again. I went to see a specialist and he asked how had I been playing football as nothing was holding my ankle in place and, in his opinion, I should give up the game.

I thought long and hard about my next move and I remember my wife was not happy with my decision and, looking back, I don't blame her, but it was something I had to do. I went to see Paul and told him to rip up my contract. I was finishing. I just couldn't sit out a three-year deal, albeit good money on the bench, or constantly in the treatment room. Looking back, I'm not sure many players would have done that but I had to be true to myself. After leaving, I was offered part-time with Doncaster Rovers, but I got into coaching which was something I really enjoyed.

My coaching career took me to Hartlepool United, where I was youth team boss, reserve boss, number two to Neale Cooper and eventually manager at the club, where I took them to within one game of the Championship after losing the play-off final. It was the furthest Hartlepool had ever got in the league. I never really enjoyed being number one – if I'm honest the perfect job for me in management was the number two job as you still had that banter with the lads and you were not responsible for players' careers like you were as the manager. So I wasn't that upset when things ended at Hartlepool.

After leaving, I worked at Bury and Middlesbrough, whilst also setting up my own successful academy around the north-east called Improtech Soccer, which delivers education in schools through football, and at present I have nine academies and it's going really well. It's a really successful tool for schools to combine the discipline and learning with football and it's also proved to be a great way into the game for lads who may have missed out on the club academy system, which I have to say is not for everyone. Also, a lot of lads are late developers, and we become invaluable to those like that as they can go on and get clubs through our coaching.

Over recent years I have had offers to come back into the game, ironically one from Bristol Rovers who appointed my old Hartlepool United mate Darrell Clarke as manager. Darrell asked me to be his number two but I declined, not only due to my academy work, but I still have a love for the red side of the city. Looking back, my time at City was certainly my best football and probably my happiest time in the game. I will always look to the club with affection and it's been a joy to talk about all my games, not only the 'Match of my Life'.

GERRY SWEENEY

Gerry Sweeney

Gerry Sweeney learnt good habits at an early age. This tough Scot's first introduction to professional football was through the mighty Glasgow Celtic under the guidance of the great Jock Stein.

After being released by Celtic as an 18-year-old, Sweeney found himself plying his trade at Scottish club Morton, where his displays in midfield alerted Bristol City's Scottish scouting network. City manager Alan Dicks paid £22,000 to bring the Scot down south, with Sweeney becoming a valuable piece of the jigsaw that would eventually become the promotion team of 1976. Sweeney's performances in midfield and full-back won the Ashton Gate faithful over in no time with his vision for a pass, tackling ability and his limitless stamina. Gerry's crowning glory was that promotion to Division One in 1976.

The best compliment paid to the likeable Scot was that he certainly did not look out of place for those four years the club spent in the top flight. Everything at the club seemed fine on the surface, until Sweeney became embroiled in the club's catastrophic fall from grace in 1982, when he, along with seven other players, were asked by the City directors to rip up their own contracts and save the club from going under. Sweeney and the rest of the seven did so, thus saving the club. The whole affair would have sent lesser men under but the tough Scot recovered and had a spell at York City, before stints in the non-league ended his playing career.

After a short spell as assistant at Walsall FC he finally came back to his beloved City as part of Joe Jordan's coaching staff, where he stayed until the appointment of new boss John Ward. There will always be affection for Gerry Sweeney at Ashton Gate, not only for his unselfish part in the Ashton Eight affair, but mainly for the 100 per cent he gave this club both on and off the field.

Bristol City 1 Portsmouth 0
Football League Division Two
20 April 1976
Ashton Gate

Bristol City: Cashley, Sweeney, Drysdale, Gow, Collier, Merrick, Tainton, Ritchie, Gillies, Cheesley, Whitehead. Sub: Mann.

Goal: Whitehead.

When I look back at my career it really is filled with ups and downs, but to be honest that is the very nature of this wonderful game. Even from an early age I realised that you could never take things for granted. I was born in Renfrew, which is about six miles outside Glasgow. Like every other boy, I wanted to play football for a living and the first port of call was Renfrew FC, which I joined. Renfrew over the years had produced a fair few footballers, like Malcolm Finlayson, who played for Millwall and Wolverhampton Wanderers in the fifties, Harry Haddock, who played for Clyde and went to the 1958 World Cup in Sweden with Scotland, and, of course, Charlie Cooke, who played for Chelsea in the seventies. I played a few games and was then spotted by Glasgow Celtic who signed me as a schoolboy.

I cannot tell you the thrill of signing for a club like Celtic – it really was a dream come true for me. The club were massive and, at the helm, was the great Jock Stein who was building a side that would eventually go on and win the European Cup. I played in a lot of reserve games but as a midfielder my path to the first team was made more difficult with the abundance of riches the club possessed in terms of my position. At the time there were Jimmy Johnstone, Bobby Murdoch, Bertie Auld, John Clark, Hugh Cunningham and young Lou Macari waiting in the wings. So it really was of no surprise when I was released as an 18-year-old along with four other midfielders at the club. Looking back, it was a privilege to have been at the club and they certainly gave me good habits that I hope I have been able to carry on, not just in my career but in life itself.

I had a few offers and signed for Morton who were in Division One. They were managed by Hal Stewart and had a good side. I think we finished sixth in my first season with the club which was no mean feat. It was at Morton that I was selected to play for the Scottish League versus the Irish League at Hampden Park. It's a game I will never forget as the feeling of pulling on my country's shirt is something that will stay with me forever. In fact, the shirt hangs in my living room to this day. We had a hell of a side that day: there was John Grieg from Rangers, my old Celtic team-mate Bobby Murdoch and Peter Cormack, who would later be a starter for both Liverpool and Bristol City. The game ended 5–2 as we were too much for the Irish League to handle, especially at Ibrox Park. It was the only time I represented Scotland but as I said, I will never forget it and it will always be right up there in terms of matches of my life.

I spent around five years at Morton when I suddenly got a call from Tony Collins, who was Bristol City's eyes and ears in Scotland. I met manager Alan Dicks and he told me they were offering £22,000 for me. I knew Morton would snap their hands off at that sort of money and I also thought about what it could mean for me and my family, so I signed. I had no clue about Bristol City but I knew they were in the Second Division and I was told it was a lovely part of England. The club were plainly going places. Chairman Harry Dolman and Alan Dicks really sold it to me. You could see that Alan was starting to build something for the future. The dressing room had a bit of experience and some fantastic youngsters coming through. The experienced lads were Ken Wimshurst, Brian Drysdale, John Galley, Dickie Rooks and Chris Garland, who was a real talent. As I said, in amongst that were youngsters of the calibre of Geoff Merrick and Keith Fear, alongside fellow Scots Tom Ritchie and Gerry Gow, who were storming through the youth team. We were a good footballing team and assistant manager John Sillett really pushed us hard in training.

I certainly won't forget my debut for City. We drew 3–3 at home to Millwall. Gerry Gow scored after three minutes, then about ten minutes later Trevor Tainton put a lovely ball into the box that I got on the end of to make it 2–0. I really could not have asked for a better start. It got the fans on my side, which thankfully never went away throughout my whole career. We finished about eighth that season and, although the club sold Chris Garland to Chelsea, you could tell we were becoming a very good side. Throughout the early seventies Alan Dicks was bringing in youngsters, as the old guard such as Ken Wimshurst, Dickie Rooks and John Galley were being moved on. Players like Clive Whitehead, Paul Cheesley and Jimmy Mann arrived, and the season before we went up we finished fifth in the league, so we knew we weren't far away, especially as prior to that we had beaten Leeds United at Elland Road in the FA Cup before being beaten by Liverpool, both teams at the time being full of star internationals.

And so to my game, and one that obviously any Bristol City fan of a certain age will remember for all their life. The match was against Portsmouth on a sunny April evening at Ashton Gate. We were up the top of the table all season fighting things out with Sunderland, West Bromwich Albion and Bolton Wanderers. Our form coming into the game wasn't great and I'm sure the supporters were a bit nervous that we might blow it. We had lost 2–1 at Blackpool, drew 1–1 at home to Chelsea and drew again 0–0 at rivals Bristol Rovers, so when it came to that warm April evening at a packed Ashton Gate we needed two points from our last two games to get promotion. So a win against George Graham's side would send us to Division One and football's top flight. Personally, after a great win against West Bromwich Albion at the Hawthorns a month earlier, I knew we could do it. When I look back on the game I have to say it wasn't a match I enjoyed, it was more a match I endured. Sure we won but there was so much at stake for us that we couldn't really enjoy the game – it was more about getting the job done.

We arrived at Ashton Gate a good few hours before kick-off and the place was buzzing then. It was a lovely evening and the ground was filling up hours before kick-off. As we went through the Ashton Gate reception, staff and supporters were wishing us well and to be honest that just added to the pressure. Alan gave us a team talk and told us to just go out and do what we had been doing all season. He told us about the fans and how we would be remembered if we pulled this off. We shook each other's hands and ran out into the evening sun. City's ground was a sea of red and white scarves. It hit me then what this would mean for all of us, supporters as well. The Portsmouth team were a very young side who had already been relegated, so in effect they had nothing to play for. They were managed by George Graham who was still turning out for them, so what I knew of George, he was going to get 100 per cent out of every one of them, youngster or not.

When you talk about massive games as this was, you always hope you can get an early goal to calm the nerves, so with about three minutes on the clock the ball went out to the right where Clive Whitehead controlled it and stuck it home. Everybody just ran towards Clive and jumped on him. It was a dream start. The whole of the ground was in uproar. I remember looking over at the dugout and Alan Dicks was moving his arms up and down to tell us to calm down and focus. Portsmouth kicked off for the restart and the noise was deafening. We got right at them but they defended brilliantly. As for us, after the initial joy of the goal, the nerves seemed to go right through the side and we were all over the place in terms of passing and doing all those things that had got us to this point through the season. To be honest I was glad when the ref blew for half-time as it gave us the chance to regroup a bit. We ran off with all the City fans singing and cheering 'We are going up'. When we got into the dressing room Alan did his best to calm us down but I think he could see on our faces the next 45 minutes was going to be tough in terms of nerves.

We went at Portsmouth in the second half and for the first 20 minutes we had numerous chances. I remember Gerry Gow going close and Paul Cheesley having a header brilliantly saved. At our end I also remember Geoff Merrick clearing a ball off our line that had the whole ground with its heart in its mouth. As the minutes ticked by you could hear the crowd getting louder and louder. In my head I just kept thinking, don't concede, don't concede. Myself and a couple of lads kept asking the ref 'How long to go?' and his reply always seemed to be 'Five minutes'. All of a sudden that was it; the ref blew and the crowd all came on. We just sprinted towards the tunnel and into the arms of all the staff that had been part of this great achievement.

When all the players were accounted for Alan told us to get up out on the grandstand and greet the fans. The feeling of jubilation is something I will never forget – everybody was hugging each other and swigging from champagne bottles. That memory as I walked out on to the grandstand and saw the whole pitch covered with supporters cheering us is something that will always stay with me. It will always be a special moment in Bristol City's history and it's a privilege that I was part of the team that did it. Alan gave a speech to the supporters and he introduced the chairman Harry Dolman who had waited his whole life for this moment to happen. We then went back to the dressing room and all jumped into the bath along with Alan Dicks, who I have to say didn't choose to jump in. The TV cameras were in there and it was absolute bedlam.

After it had all died down we went away to Spain together to reflect on the fantastic season we had had. Liverpool were staying in the same hotel as us and the banter was brilliant, especially as we, like Liverpool, were a Division One club now. Reflecting on the season, we had won promotion through our away form, which had been phenomenal, and the team had a spirit that was unshakeable. We were there for each other on and off the field. Moments like that night in 1976 don't happen very often in the game so you have to savour them. It was a very proud night for me and that's why it will always be the 'Match of my Life'.

Looking back, we did well in the top flight. We lasted four seasons and we matched every side we played against. I don't think we were ever really outplayed or taken apart. Unfortunately relegation came at the start of the eighties. It cost Alan Dicks his job and it was the start of a catastrophic time for the club. Bob Houghton replaced Alan Dicks and he could not stop the club being relegated again into the third tier of the Football League. Houghton was then replaced mid-season with Roy Hodgson and it was during this time that things came to a head for everybody.

We had just played Aston Villa in the FA Cup when some of the lads got envelopes, which none of us really paid too much attention to. The next morning I was cleaning my car when I got a call for me to come to the ground immediately. I told them I had to get changed but they said get here now. When I arrived at the ground I thought it was a joke. I went into reception and the first person I saw was Chris Garland who had come back to the club a few years prior. Knowing that Chris loved a joke I was starting to think this was a setup. He then said to me, 'You have got the job haven't you.' I told him I had no idea what was going on. We were then taken into the boardroom where a director came in and told us 'Take it or leave it'. I responded by saying, 'Take or leave what?' He then said, 'Have they not told you?' I shook my head and he pointed out that the club were around £800,000 in debt and to save it we had to basically rip up our contracts as we were the top earners. In the room were me, Geoff Merrick, Chris Garland, Peter Aitken, Julian Marshall, David Rodgers, Jimmy Mann and Trevor Tainton. We just looked at each other in disbelief as we had no clue, and I certainly didn't as I didn't get an envelope with it all in.

I told Geoff to phone the PFA right away which he did. They told us to stay put and accept nothing until their secretary Gordon Taylor had met us. We talked for hours and thought about the supporters, and if we didn't agree we would be letting them down, but on the other hand we all had mortgages and families. We were put in a terrible position, and in the end we agreed to save the club. When I look back it was a dreadful way to end our careers at the club. I had four months left on my contract so I just got my things and left.

Peter Aitken and I went and played a few games at York City till the end of the season. After that I played non-league with Forest Green Rovers and Gloucester City for a few seasons. I then got into coaching after a call from Tommy Coakley who I had played with at Morton. Tommy was manager at Walsall and I went as his assistant for a while. Things went well there as we finished eighth in the Third Division, but I wanted to get back to Bristol, which I did and got a job as a postman, thinking that I was finished with the game, until I got a call from Bristol City assistant Jimmy Lumsden who I had been at Celtic with. He asked me if I would be interested in being part of his backroom staff, working with the youngsters and doing some scouting for the club. I agreed straightaway as I was pleased to come back to the club despite the circumstances of my leaving. I enjoyed my time and, when Jimmy left the club for pastures new, I worked closely with new manager Joe Jordan and became his assistant.

This time in my life throws up another game I remember as I am the only Bristol City manager with a 100 per cent record. Yes, it's true. We were due to play Crewe Alexandra away and unfortunately we had had some bad results that led to Joe being sacked on the Monday night. He phoned me to tell me and minutes later one of the directors called and asked me to take control of the game away at Crewe. Obviously I said yes, but I never really had any great ambitions to go into management, so I was realistic about the task ahead. I came away from the call and thought about how I had now ended up manager at the club, and I promised myself that for however long this was going to last I was going to enjoy it. So I took the team at Gresty Road and I was very proud to be manager of the club that I loved. I changed a few things around that myself and Joe had talked about and it was great to come away 2–1 winners with Junior Bent and Shaun Goater doing the business for me. That evening I was told that John Ward would be coming in as manager straightaway. John brought his own men in and in the nature of the game I left City for the second time.

Today I am retired and keep myself fit. I go to a few games and get a great response from the fans who always talk about the evening game against Portsmouth and what it meant to them. Many tell me that they were on the pitch looking up at us and how proud of us they were, which is a lovely thing to say. That side were a special team; we were like brothers on and off the field. We may not have been full of skilled individuals but we worked hard and at times played hard. They will always be special to me as we achieved something that I don't even think the supporters dreamed we could do. It's great to see that the team means as much to the fans as they mean to me.

BOB TAYLOR

Bob Taylor

Bob Taylor was the centre-forward the Bristol City fans had been dreaming about since the days of the great John Atyeo. When manager Joe Jordan paid Leeds United £225,000 for this Leeds United reserve in 1988, little did they know Jordan had uncovered a gem who would be loved by the City fans forever. Taylor had many attributes from speed to bravery, but the main one was just scoring goals – he had a knack for it that just could not be taught. A member of City's 1989/90 Third Division promotion side, Taylor's contribution was immense with 27 league goals. It was plain that Taylor's exploits would catch the eye of other clubs, and in the 1991/92 season City sold their gem to West Bromwich Albion for £300,000. At the Hawthorns he would go on to have cult status with the fans as he did with City. Later moves to Bolton Wanderers and Cheltenham Town never ceased his appetite for goals. He was a player who always gave 100 per cent for the red shirt and that, besides his scoring exploits, will always keep him in the hearts of the Ashton Gate fans.

Bristol City 3 Chelsea 1
FA Cup fourth round
27 January 1990
Ashton Gate

Bristol City: Sinclair, Llewellyn, Bailey, Shelton, Humphries, Rennie, Gavin, Newman, Taylor, Smith, Turner. Subs: Miller, Mellon.

Goals: Turner 2, Gavin.

When I was asked about remembering one game in the City shirt it's quite funny that I never thought about one in which I scored, but the first game that came to me was the FA Cup tie against Chelsea at Ashton Gate. I have always loved the FA Cup ever since I was a kid. I think it's the best cup competition in the world and it was always my dream to play in a final. Unfortunately the closest I got was a semi-final defeat against Stoke City in 2011 when I was playing for Bolton Wanderers. This game at Ashton Gate really did capture the fans' imagination and for us we were ecstatic when the draw was made and we were home to Chelsea.

We had done really well in the previous rounds, knocking out Barnet in the first round then beating Fulham 2–1 at home, before beating local rivals Swindon Town 2–1 again at Ashton Gate. I had scored in every round and I had about 17 goals already that season, so I was really full of confidence, as we all were to be fair, particularly after the Swindon Town game as they were riding high in the league and we really did a job on them. The build-up to the game was really intense regarding local media, but I don't think nationally people thought there was going to be an upset. Chelsea were doing well in the league and their side was full of internationals like Graham Roberts, Kerry Dixon, David Speedie and Graeme Le Saux, and they could all look after themselves. I remember getting to the ground and although the weather was terrible the fans were in great voice. Chelsea had brought a few thousand along the M4 with them and they were packed into the old open end.

When we went out for the warm-up you could just feel the tension from both sets of supporters as they were slinging insults back and forth. The game was televised and was going to be on that night's *Match of the Day* but I think the result would certainly decide where it came in the running order. Our manager Joe Jordan just said to us not to be fearful and go out and get stuck into them. He told us with the rain pouring down they just might not fancy it this afternoon so we had to be on top of our game and ready to exploit any weakness they might show. The rain was absolutely lashing down and I, for one, couldn't wait for the game to start.

When it did, it was a very cagey affair. We were very definite with any passing as we knew that if we didn't strike the ball properly it would get stuck in the pitch and cause ourselves problems. Myself and Robbie Turner up front were just starting to get stuck into Graham Roberts and Ken Monkou and they were giving it back when the ball fell to full-back Andy Llewellyn on the edge of the box. Andy isn't known for his shooting but he cracked a beauty from all of 25 yards that went through a wall of players. Chelsea keeper Dave Beasant saw it late and it bounced just out of his grasp and fell at my feet. Nine times out of ten I would have tapped it into the goal but for some reason I thought I would smash it home and with that I completely missed the ball and almost took Beasant's head clean off. It's something I will always remember as I have no idea what I was thinking. If I had connected with Beasant I would have been sent off and we would have been a man down after five minutes and this would have been a completely different story I would be telling. Thankfully Robbie was at my side and he did what I should have, and that was tap the ball home to put us 1–0 up. Ashton Gate went crazy. The goal was in front of the East End and you got a sense that maybe something special was on the cards. The weather never really made for a great match but when we went in at half-time 1–0 up we were overjoyed. In the dressing room we could all hear the noise from the crowd outside and, coming off, a few of the Chelsea players looked a bit rattled. We had done everything Joe had asked of us. We were on the front foot, we pushed and squeezed them, and myself and Robbie held the ball up and caused them all sorts of problems.

We started the second half just how we had ended the first. We had a few long-range shots and Robbie was having a stormer alongside me. Then with about 20 minutes left, Dave Smith went down the line and crossed to me. I turned Chelsea defender Ken Monkou and played the ball to Gary Shelton on the edge of the six-yard box. Instead of shooting, Gary played a ball sideways to Robbie and he stuck it in off the post to make it 2–0. We knew then that this was going to be our afternoon. The City fans went wild with some of them racing on to the pitch. After eventually clearing the fans we knew that this was going to be a very long

20 minutes as Chelsea came back at us. With about ten minutes on the board they got one back through a Kevin Wilson header. Our heads never dropped and with five minutes left we got a free kick inside our half. John Bailey whacked it upfield and Robbie held on to it then turned the defence and shot. Keeper Beasant could only push the ball out and Mark Gavin arrived to make it 3–1 and win us the tie.

The scenes at the end were incredible. The City fans were going crazy and the Chelsea fans started to dismantle the open end of Ashton Gate, throwing bits of advertising hoardings on to the pitch. The result was the big upset that weekend and we all phoned each other that night as we found out it was to be the main game on *Match of the Day*. Things like that were great for us and the fans. I was really proud to see Bristol City in the national spotlight and the Sunday papers were full of it too. As I said, I played in loads of games with City but that one match sticks with me as it was a great team effort with a great bunch of lads who, if we had stayed together, could really have gone on and achieved something. Our FA Cup exploits, though, ended in the next round when we were beaten by Cambridge United.

When I look at my career, I started at Leeds United and they taught me good habits, but it was Bristol City where I became a player. I was born in a small mining town called Horden in County Durham. I am extremely thankful to Margaret Thatcher for closing the local colliery as my dad had my name down to join, which I wasn't too keen on. I played football for Horden Colliery, which was men's football, and managed by Dickie Malone who played for Sunderland in the 1973 Cup Final. It was Dickie who got me a trial at Leeds United and where my football education started. Leeds were managed by Billy Bremner and he was a true legend on and off the pitch. He would give you so much advice and he had all us apprentices captivated with his tales of the Don Revie era. I progressed through the ranks and became top scorer in the reserves, but then Billy was sacked and Howard Wilkinson came to the club. Howard had a plan for the side which in hindsight worked as they won the league a few years later but he wanted to bring his own players in and that meant selling some of the youngsters, one of which was me.

There had been a bit of interest from different clubs but Bristol City were very keen and they had Joe Jordan as manager and that went a long way with me. Joe had also sounded Billy Bremner out about me and he was nothing but glowing regarding what I could do. I didn't know anything about Bristol but Joe picked me up and drove me down to have a look round. We actually did the deal in the physio room without any agents or anything. Joe said the money was this and I signed there and then. I went back up north to get my stuff then came straight back. I think the fee was £225,000 which to me was huge, but I gained so much confidence from the fact that Joe Jordan rated me. I came back to Bristol and the first players I bumped into were Rob Newman and Glenn Humphries. Joe told them that they were to look after me and they did on and off the pitch. The whole place just felt right and I hit the ground running.

I made my debut in an away game at Bristol Rovers and the atmosphere was brilliant. I never realised the extent of the rivalry between the two clubs, although I don't have the fondest memories about playing Rovers. I'm particularly talking about a game we won 1–0 at Ashton Gate when I was accused along with Andy Llewellyn and Rob Newman of making a gesture to the visiting Rovers fans after we had scored. I was livid as it cost me a £650 FA fine and I had not done anything. It got worse when Andy and Rob were both found not guilty, only for Andy to admit he did it weeks later. I could have killed him.

I loved my time at City and Joe really took me under his wing and taught me so much, just like Billy Bremner had done at Leeds. Joe was a mine of information about being a striker, his time in Italy, nutrition and looking after yourself. I'm sure that's why my career lasted so long, due to Joe's advice. We won promotion in the 1989/90 season and I was named player of the year mainly due to my 34 goals in league and cup, but we were still disappointed at losing out to Rovers for the championship. We started the next season well but then Joe left to manage Hearts in Scotland and I was devastated.

Jimmy Lumsden took over and, although Jim was a good number two, he was certainly no number one. Jim liked to switch forwards around which was okay but I was injured and at that time my mum had passed away, so I was all over the place in terms of personal stuff. What I really needed was a manager who was going to give me some confidence, arm round the shoulder stuff, which was what I thrived on, but unfortunately that was not Jimmy. Then out of the blue an offer came from West Bromwich Albion. I mulled it over and thought, well, maybe it might just be the right time to leave. I know that if Joe was still at the club I would have stayed a few more years but I think in my heart of hearts I knew it was probably the right time to go.

Bobby Gould signed me in a deal worth £300,000 and again things went really well for me at Albion. Bobby was a real one-off. The fans hated him. I don't know whether it was his links to Wolves who he used to play for or just his style, but they were relentless in their dislike for him. I remember going to Shrewsbury Town once and we were not doing that well in the league and the fans brought a coffin and passed it around the whole of the ground to symbolise Bobby getting the sack. He did make me laugh, though. I remember he wanted to bring in some of the things he used at Wimbledon to try and get us going. Once he put a boxing ring up and, with all the lads and apprentices lined around the ring, he got in with his gloves on and asked who fancied having a go with him? We were not doing that well at that particular time and we were leaking goals non-stop. I think Bobby wanted to try and bring us all together. Anyway, striker

Colin West, who wasn't keen on Bobby's methods, grabbed the gloves and said, 'I will have a go.' Within minutes Colin gave Bobby an upper cut that stuck him on his back. When Bobby came round he looked at all the lads and said, 'See how important it is to have a good defence.' The whole place just erupted with laughter. In the end the fans had their way and Bobby was sacked. It's quite flattering now when I go back to Albion and the fans say the best thing Bobby Gould ever did was sign Bob Taylor but, as I said, I liked him.

A few managers came and went at the Hawthorns and I just kept on scoring like I had done at Bristol City and the fans, again like City's, just loved it. It wasn't all plain sailing, though. I got injured towards the end of the season and missed the preseason, so I was playing catch-up with the lads when new manager Denis Smith arrived. After a week, Denis told me I was overweight, unfit and I liked a drink. I was not happy at all. I was obviously a bit overweight due to the injury and that's why I wasn't as fit as the rest of the lads, but as for drinking, it certainly wasn't a culture at the club. Denis said he wanted me to go out on loan so he could see me play. I told him I wasn't prepared to go on loan and would play in the reserves and then get in the first team, but Denis was having none of it. He even told me that I should go out on loan at Oxford United where he had just been manager. No disrespect to Oxford but he knew what I could do, and I could do it at a higher level than Oxford.

In the end the stalemate went on and on before I got a call from Colin Todd at Premiership side Bolton Wanderers asking if I would be interested in coming for the tail end of the season. I snapped his hand off and ended up getting my first Premiership goal away at Manchester United. It's funny, looking back, that Smith wouldn't play me in a Championship game but was happy for me to go and play Premiership football. It was a really sad way for me to leave Albion at that time but things were a bit personal with me and Smith and, like the move away from Bristol City, it just seemed the right time to leave even though I was gutted.

In the end I moved to Bolton after the loan period and I enjoyed my time there under Colin Todd, then Sam Allardyce. The fans took to me and I got to two cup semi-finals with them. After a couple of seasons, I went back to West Brom under Gary Megson on a three-year deal, which really suited me. I eventually hung up my boots after spells at Cheltenham Town, under Bobby Gould, Tamworth and Kidderminster Harriers. It was difficult to finish playing as it was all I ever knew but the memories I took away were priceless. Today I keep myself fit and healthy by working in the real world where I fit mezzanine flooring all over the country. I always get a good reception from the fans at all the clubs I played for, but there will always be a special place for my time at Bristol City. As I said, it was a period in my life where I was just married and starting a family, that combined with just starting to get to grips with being a footballer. The fans must also take a lot of credit for the way they treated me during my time at Ashton Gate. I was a confidence player and they gave me a boost every time I ran out to represent the club. The feeling I got from them will always be very dear to me.

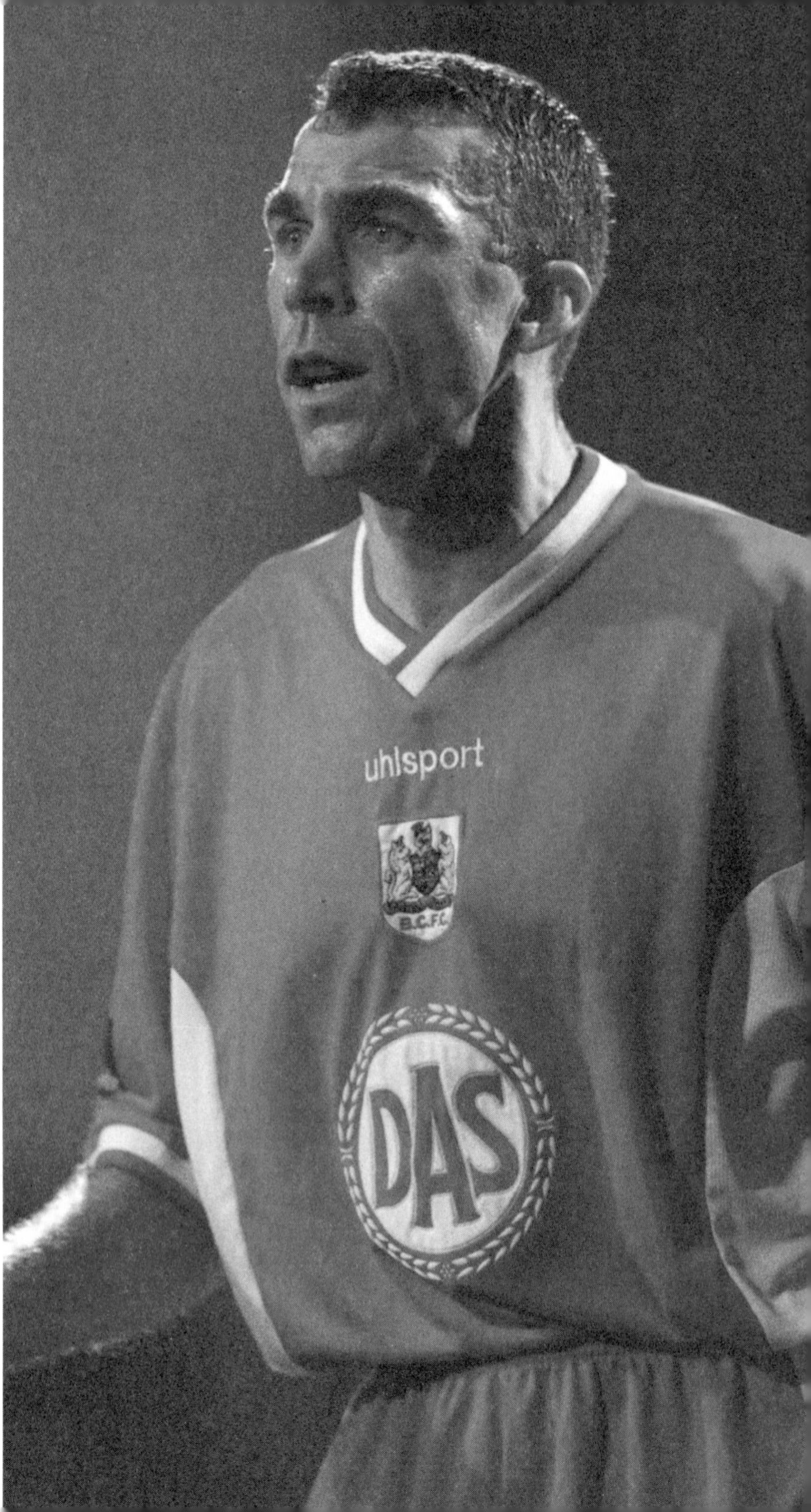

SHAUN TAYLOR

Shaun Taylor

Shaun Taylor arrived at Ashton Gate in 1996 and he was certainly a player with a point to prove. At the age of 33 this colossus of a centre-half was found to be surplus to requirements at Swindon Town where manager Steve McMahon had taken over the reins. Swindon's loss certainly proved to be Bristol City's gain as Joe Jordan shrewdly snapped up the West Country stopper, who would go on to be one of the Ashton Gate fans' favourites. Taylor came to professional football late in life after playing non-league and qualifying as a plumber, and it was Exeter City that gave the Plymouth-born player his chance, which he grabbed with both hands, becoming captain of the club during their 1989 promotion to Division Three. A move to Swindon Town under the guidance of manager Glenn Hoddle made Taylor a cult figure amongst the Swindon fans, where he was a part of the side that won promotion to the Premier League in the 1992/93 season. Taylor embraced football's top flight, playing every one of their games and scoring 13 goals in the process. So it was plain to see that many fans were shocked when he was shown the door by McMahon and sold for £50,000. A move along the M4 certainly got his career back on track.

Shaun was truly an 'old school' type of player who would put his head in where it hurts, and never shied away from a challenge. He forged a brilliant partnership with the young Louis Carey in the heart of the City defence that would go on and clinch promotion in the 1997/98 season under John Ward. At the age of 35 he sustained a ruptured cruciate ligament in a game against Watford. It was an injury that would have finished many a career, but ten months later Taylor returned to the City side just as determined as before. Shaun played 126 games for Bristol City before he begrudgingly retired through injury in 2000. A keen coach, he joined the backroom staff at Ashton Gate, working with the reserves until 2005 when he left the club. He became assistant manager at Forest Green Rovers but left to join his old club Exeter City as youth team coach in 2009. Today Shaun is assistant manager to ex-Bristol City boss Gary Johnson at Torquay United. Taylor will always be held in high regard by the City faithful. He was a player who gave everything for the shirt and surely that is the highest accolade any player could be given.

Bristol City 4 Grimsby Town 1
Football League Division Two
10 January 1998
Ashton Gate

Bristol City: Welch, Locke, Bell, Goodridge, Taylor, Carey, Edwards, Doherty, Goater, Cramb, Tinnion. Subs: Murray, Hewlett, Torpey.

Goals: Cramb 2, Taylor, Goater.

I was lucky with my career. I always had a real affinity with the supporters of every club I played for. I suppose I always thought that I was doing what they all wanted to do and play for their club, so I knew that the position I was in came with a certain amount of responsibility. I have certainly had some ups and downs in the game, and I suppose looking back over my time at Bristol City I can recall two games that sum that up perfectly. One was where I got injured and really thought I may not be able to get back into the side and the other was a match where we as a side never put a foot wrong.

My road to Ashton Gate is much like any other footballer, although I did arrive at the professional game late in comparison with some players. I think this only served to make me enjoy it and value it more. I was at Plymouth Argyle as a youngster and they were my hometown club. My dad was a big fan and when I wasn't playing for the youth team we would go to Home Park and watch them play. To be a player was all I ever wanted to do, so when I was released as a 16-year-old it really was devastating for me, especially when they told me I wasn't big enough. I had a long chat with my dad and he advised me to go and get a trade, which I did in plumbing. Being down in the West Country it's such a big area but without many clubs, so it wasn't as if there were too many options for me to find another club, and to be honest I lost a little bit of love for the game at that time.

I continued with the plumbing work and played part-time with St Blazey, before moving on to Bideford Town where I did really well and came to the notice of Exeter City. They put a bid in and that was the turning point for me. I was in my twenties at this time and grabbed the opportunity with both hands. We had a decent team and were managed by Terry Cooper, who made us play some good football. A few people wondered if I would be able to cope with the demands of league football, but I became captain and my career at Exeter was topped off with winning the Fourth Division title in 1989. There was interest from other clubs and Terry never stood in my way, as I wanted to get on in my playing career as I felt I had missed out a bit starting so late.

Swindon Town came in for me and the fee was £200,000, which was a lot for Exeter to receive and a lot for Swindon to pay. I know now that Swindon's assistant manager John Gorman really had to convince manager Glenn Hoddle to sign me as I don't think I was Glenn's cup of tea. But credit to John, he battled away and I ended up signing and even taking the place of Argentinian World Cup star Nestor Lorenzo's place in the side. I loved my time at Swindon. We had a good side with the likes of Fitzroy Simpson, Colin Calderwood and Paul Bodin, not to mention Glenn Hoddle, who was still playing and was fantastic with the ball. We won promotion to the Premier League and I never missed a game all season and even scored 13 goals in the process.

But with that success came the call from Chelsea, and Glenn left along with a few of the players. John took over but we struggled in the top flight and were relegated the following season. Steve McMahon took over and, although I had a year on my contract and was in my thirties, he thought my legs had gone so I never featured in his plans. I am the sort of bloke that it's all about playing, so if I'm not picked I might as well go elsewhere. My prayers were answered when Joe Jordan bid £50,000 for me to come to Bristol City. To be honest it was a dream move for me as they are the biggest side in the south-west and I had a perfect opportunity to prove people wrong again, despite my age.

I have nothing but great memories of my time at City. I made my debut against Shrewsbury Town away. We lost 1–0 and Joe was under pressure to get results. In the end he was replaced through the season with John Ward, who I really liked. At the end of that season I was named player of the year which was such a thrill considering all the doubt about me at Swindon. We finished the season in the play-offs but were beaten by Brentford. We were all disappointed but we knew we would give it a right go the following season. We had a really talented side under John, with myself and a young Louis Carey at the back, helped by Brian Tinnion, Tommy Doherty and Mickey Bell. The side had a great mixture of experience and youngsters who were fearless.

The one 'Match of my Life' that sticks in my mind was in the January of our promotion season. We were neck and neck with Watford as to who was going to go up. We had gone on a good run before the Christmas but we had lost our previous game 1–0 away at Fulham who were in the top six, so we really needed a good performance against Grimsby, who themselves were fourth in the league going into the game and were coming off the back of a 13-game unbeaten run. There was a lot of talk of how City would blow the run-in and maybe end up in the play-offs, but that was clearly not how we felt. It was a bitterly cold Ashton Gate with about 15,000 crammed in. The atmosphere was a bit low key as I'm sure the City fans were worried about how we would fare, particularly after our defeat at Fulham. We kicked off and really hit the ground running when Greg Goodridge went down the wing to test their full-back and he put in a cracking cross for Colin Cramb to hit and the ball went in off the post. I think the goal was timed at about 17 seconds. It was a great start and we just got better and better. Five minutes later a perfect free kick from Brian Tinnion's left foot picked me out and I dived to put us 2–0 up. That really was my game when it came to heading. I only ever was focused on the ball, so although people used to say I was brave I really just followed the ball and tried to get my head on the end of it.

There were about six minutes gone and we were 2–0 up. Ashton Gate was buzzing and the 15,000 crowd sounded like 50,000. All the prematch nerves had gone and we were playing like a side destined to gain promotion. I remember everything we did came off. We were battering their goal and Brian Tinnion was unbelievable that afternoon, spraying the ball around the pitch like I used to see Glenn Hoddle do. Brian was a real talent. Just before half-time Colin Cramb got on the end of a fantastic move involving Louis Carey, Mickey Bell and Greg Goodridge. Colin slipped the ball past the Grimsby keeper to put us 3–0 up at half-time. When we walked off the whole of Ashton Gate stood and applauded us. I will never forget that feeling of pride I had for myself and my fellow pros. I have certainly never felt that at half-time before. John patted us all on the back as we came into the dressing room and Crammy was asking what his goal was timed at as he had heard a national newspaper were offering £3,000 for the quickest goal. I still don't know if he won it.

We were delighted to hear that our main rivals Watford were losing, so as it stood we were top of the league. As we came out, the fans let us know as they sang 'We are top of the league, say we are top of the league'. We had more chances with Tommy Doherty going close before Brian Tinnion beat off two players to slip the ball to Shaun Goater who made it 4–0. Grimsby got one back late on, which I was not happy about, but we came off the pitch to a rousing standing ovation. I have played in lots of sides that have won titles but that day was perfect in every way. We were unstoppable, we helped each other, supported each other and tore what was a very good Grimsby side apart. We were singing and shouting in the dressing room as Watford had lost and we were top. Our chairman Scott Davidson sent in crates of champagne, but it showed the discipline and focus of the side that we agreed we would not touch it until we had secured promotion.

We all but secured promotion that season when we went to Oldham and won 2–1 in the March. For me, though, the season will always be tinged with a bit of sadness as we went to Watford's Vicarage Road in the April in what was billed as a title decider. We drew the game 1–1, but I remember in the first half going up for a ball with the Watford keeper, who if I remember was called Chamberlain, and as I came down I felt something go in my leg. I struggled on until half-time and had some treatment. I knew something was wrong but I carried on for a bit of the second half before coming off. I was sent to a specialist who told me that I had ruptured my cruciate ligament. It was a massive blow, not only to miss the last couple of games that were in a promotion-winning season, but bearing in mind my age, I did wonder if I would get back again.

We finished the season second to Watford and me on crutches doing my best to enjoy the promotion party, although winning the player of the year again really helped me in what was going to be a long road to recovery. I was now about 34 years of age and it was really tough missing that season in Division One, but I worked so hard in rehab and it was hell watching the lads in training and on matchdays. I was out for ten months and, in that time, John had been replaced by Benny Lennartsson who had arrived from Danish club

Lyngby. But the side struggled with Benny as he was new to British football.

My return was a home game against Port Vale in which we won 2–1. I had a fantastic reception from the fans, with many of them telling me they never thought they would see me return to full fitness. The win was our first of the new year but relegation was on the cards. I played the last eight games of the season but we finished bottom of the league. Benny was replaced, and in the summer Tony Pulis was in place as manager. I know the City fans are not keen on Pulis's time at the club but for me he was brilliant as he taught me so much about defending – it really improved my game.

I played on the next season but I was finding it difficult and, after Pulis left, Danny Wilson arrived with Frank Barlow. They offered me the chance to go into the coaching of the reserves, which I loved. It was a dream come true to still be involved in the game after retirement. I stayed with city working under Danny and then Brian Tinnion, but left in 2005 when Gary Johnson arrived with his own backroom staff. I went to Forest Green Rovers as Gary Owers's assistant and I loved that, before moving to Exeter City as youth team boss under Paul Tisdale. My career has also taken me back to Plymouth for a stint as youth team boss, before finding me at the moment, assistant at Torquay United to, would you believe, Gary Johnson.

My time at City is very special to me. My footballing career is full of people who may doubt your ability, and that, like it or lump it, is the nature of the game – it's all about opinions. I like to think I ended up changing a few people's opinions of me along the way. The 'Match of my Life' was without doubt one of the best team displays I ever played in and that set of lads' skill and team spirit that day and that season will live with me a long time. It was a joy to be part of and thank you for letting me look back on it.

BRIAN TINNION

Brian Tinnion

Brian Tinnion was one of the most skilful and gifted players ever to pull on the red shirt of Bristol City. The likeable Geordie arrived at the club in 1993 from Bradford City and, looking back, the £180,000 fee seems peanuts to what this skilful midfielder brought to the club. In Tinnion, the Ashton Gate fans had a new hero, and not necessarily one who scored goals, although he had his share, but one who became the very heart of the team, a player who could create something special with a genius pass for those around him. Brian's playing career at City lasted some 12 years and in that time he was part of a team that won promotion in the 1997/98 season and also lifted the LDV Trophy in 2003. It's testament to his professionalism that he was a regular throughout that time. In 2005, following the play-off final defeat to Brighton, manager Danny Wilson was sacked and Brian was offered the Bristol City hot seat. Although Tinnion started well, he soon became aware that the job had come too soon for him. After a savage 7–1 defeat at Swansea City, Brian resigned and moved to Spain. He returned in 2013 to head up Bristol City's Academy and recruitment and together the club and Brian have never looked back, producing the next generation of City stars.

Liverpool 0 Bristol City 1
FA Cup third round replay
25 January 1994
Anfield

Bristol City: Welch, Llewellyn, Scott, Shail, Munro, Tinnion, Martin, Bent, Robinson, Allison, Edwards. Subs: Pennyfather, Rosenior, Leaning.

Goal: Tinnion.

My journey to Bristol City started with me watching Newcastle United from the Gallowgate End at St James' Park. I had always dreamed of being a footballer and it was a dream come true to eventually play for Newcastle. I was part of the FA Youth Cup-winning side of 1985 that also included Paul Gascoigne. The manager was Jack Charlton and he really believed in giving youngsters a chance in the first team. I played about 30 games for United as a full-back but, when Charlton was sacked, Jim Smith came in and he wanted experience in all positions, so I found myself looking for a club. I was disappointed and Jim was a good bloke, but I didn't want to sit in the reserves.

I had two offers, one from Bradford City and one from Middlesbrough, but Bradford at the time were in a higher division so I signed for them under manager Terry Yorath, who really sold the club to me. I had four great years at Bradford but my contract was up and suddenly I got an offer from Bristol City, who had been watching me for ages apparently. I met manager Russell Osman and his scout Tony Fawthrop and I liked what they had to say. I came down to Bristol and something about the place just felt right. The ground was great and there were good people around the club, so I signed. I think the fee was set by tribunal at about £180,000, although I never felt any real pressure by it. So that was the start of my love affair with this great club.

Over the years I have played in some wonderful games. I remember when I did sign the dressing room was pretty down as City were in a relegation dogfight along with neighbours Bristol Rovers, so everyone was under pressure, particularly the management. We then played Bristol Rovers in the league at Ashton Gate and I remember there were about 25,000 in the ground with loads locked out; it was incredible. That's when I knew how big this game was and how important this derby was to the people of Bristol. I remember being 1–0 up through Wayne Allison and then we got a penalty. Our penalty taker Martin Scott was suspended so everybody just looked at each other, so I picked up the ball and took it. I had taken penalties before at Bradford so it was no problem. I stuck it past the keeper and the ground went crazy. I think, looking back, that was the moment when the City fans took me into their hearts. I think they admired the way I took responsibility of the situation. I also think it could have gone horribly wrong had I missed, but in the end we won 2–1 and stayed up that year as Rovers were relegated.

I suppose the game that I will always be remembered for, though, will be that famous night in the club's history when we beat Liverpool 1–0 at Anfield. It was a really strange build-up to the game. We were drawn against them at home in the third round of the FA Cup and Ashton Gate was packed to the rafters. The game was really even and we gave a good account of ourselves. We had about 20 minutes of the game left with the score at 1–1 and suddenly the floodlights failed, so the game was rescheduled for the following week and again we gave a good account of ourselves, and to be honest we could have beaten them. In the end we drew 1–1 so off to Anfield we went.

I think deep down we thought our chance had gone and I know the media thought that as they really didn't give us a prayer. In fact, nobody did. After all, we were mid-table in Division One and this was Liverpool with all their stars at Anfield. As players we just went out to give it our best shot, work hard and enjoy the night. We had a game plan, though. Manager Russell Osman and his assistant Tony Fawthrop told me to come inside more towards big centre-forward Wayne Allison. This would mean we would get more of the ball and I would get anything that Wayne knocked down around the box. When we ran out it was incredible. City had taken over 10,000 fans and the noise both sets of supporters made was deafening. As I said, we really felt relaxed and I remember taking it all in. Anfield was a special place under floodlights and I hoped they lasted for 90 minutes.

We really got at them right from the off and we knew if we let them play their passing game they would hurt us so we just didn't give them any time on the ball. They had two chances early on, but our keeper Keith Welch coped with them and that gave us even more confidence. The game was pretty much end to end with us having a chance with Wayne Allison, and Martin Scott clearing off our line from John Barnes. I remember Barnes getting the better of Stuart Munro and cutting inside to shoot and his effort was brilliantly saved by Keith in goal. It's really funny looking back but the longer the game went on I really didn't feel they would score. Our full-backs Andy Llewellyn and Martin Scott had the better of Steve McManaman and Mark Walters on their wings and they and the fans became more and more frustrated as the game went on. I remember Souness shouting to the wingers 'Take them on, take them on', but they just didn't. I put a great ball in from a free kick and Wayne Allison forced a great save from Bruce Grobbelaar in the Liverpool goal. Again it just inspired us. With about 15 minutes left in the first half I had a great chance to score when Wayne Allison set me up but I stuck it wide, much to the relief of the Liverpool fans who were not happy that we were still in the game. We went in at half-time full of confidence.

They came out second half with McManaman switching wings, but again our defence were heroic. We had chance after chance and I remember their keeper Bruce Grobbelaar handling the ball from outside the box when pressed by Junior Bent but the ref just gave a yellow card instead of a red. We were all incensed by the decision but we kept going. Then in the 67th minute the moment happened that will always be linked with my career at City. Allison ran through the middle but was thwarted by Liverpool defender Neil Ruddock. It just span out to me and I hit it with my left foot. From the moment it left my boot I knew it was in. I just went crazy – all the lads were jumping on top of me and the fact that it was in front of the Kop was a dream. They came at us but our defence just stood firm until the end.

The scenes at the final whistle were incredible. The Liverpool players couldn't wait to get off the pitch as the boos rang out around them but the whole of the Kop end stayed and gave us a standing ovation, which shows the class of those supporters. We did a lap of honour and our fans were incredible, throwing hats and scarves on to the pitch for us. I really didn't want to come off. In the dressing room after, it was just chaos with us singing, dancing and drinking champagne. Neil Ruddock came in to wish us all the best and also give us a crate of beer, which was a nice touch from him. I got the man of the match award but our whole team deserved it – they were immense.

We returned to Bristol as heroes and were the main talking point across Britain's media for a while. The repercussions for Liverpool were that they sacked manager Graeme Souness the next day, which was a sad way for the Liverpool legend to leave the club. For us we were back to the league, winning our next game 2–0 at home to Tranmere Rovers, with myself and Wayne Allison getting the goals. Our cup run saw us go to Stockport County in the next round where we won 4–0, but the dream ended in the fifth round, losing 2–0 to Charlton Athletic after a replay. As for the season, we finished mid-table, but what a night that was. I never get tired of reliving it with fans as you get to see how important it was to them.

During my time at City I was always interested in coaching and particularly bringing on the youngsters. I used to work at the academy on an evening while I was still playing for the first team. I really thrived on it and enjoyed that side of things under manager Danny Wilson. I had a great relationship with Danny. I became a bit of a father figure in the side for the younger lads and also became a bit of a buffer in between the manager and the lads. He trusted me a lot and if he couldn't get to a local function I would go instead, which I really enjoyed. Then after our defeat against Brighton in the play-off final, a game where we just didn't show up for whatever reason, Danny was released the following morning.

The next thing I knew was a phone call from chairman Steve Lansdown asking me if I wanted the job. I thought long and hard about it and the only thing that worried me was whether I would ever get the chance again. I spoke to Danny who told me how tough it would be, but I thought I couldn't turn it down. It was hard, all those lads in the dressing room who were my mates. I was now the boss and I struggled a bit at first with that. Looking back at my time in charge, I am really proud that we finished seventh in my first season and also I gave seven debuts to lads who went on to have good careers in the game. But if I'm honest, yes, the job came too soon for me and it all culminated one afternoon at Swansea City. We had terrible injuries and had to play half the youth team. We competed for about 40 minutes before they got their first goal and after that we just fell apart due to us having no leaders in the side. In the end we lost 7–1 and I knew it was all over for me. I told Steve Lansdown, and he pleaded with me telling me that I would weather the storm. He said he would give me whatever I needed but what I needed at that time was a break.

I resigned and kept fit training with Cheltenham Town, before deciding to move to Spain with my family where I ran soccer schools for Charlton Athletic, whilst also becoming Everton's Spanish scout covering all levels of the Spanish leagues. I enjoyed it but I think there was a burning hole in me that wanted to get back into the game. The break away from the game recharged my batteries but I knew it was not going to be a long-term thing. As luck would have it, my family and I were thinking of coming back to the UK when I got a call from City directors Keith Dawe and Jon Lansdown in 2013 asking me if I would be interested in coming back to the club to run the academy and recruitment. It was a no-brainer for me and the family as we loved the city and I loved the club. It was a role that I knew would suit me as I had good habits from my Newcastle days that I could draw on when working with the youngsters, and I had worked with the academy before so I knew the setup.

When I arrived, the setup certainly needed an overhaul as Bristol lads were being picked up by Aston Villa, Cardiff and Southampton, and that had to change.

I worked closely with the scouts and worked with the youngsters and made sure their families were happy, and after time, we now have the pick of any player in the area and know about all of them. The club's philosophy regarding youngsters helps as well as Lee Johnson and myself talk constantly about the players we have coming through, and we do have some fantastic youngsters just underneath the first team who go out on loan for experience, and I watch their progress every game they play and report back to the manager. We feel that if, say, we have a midfielder who is 18 months away from being ready for the first team and Lee needs a midfielder, we will sign one but only for 18 months. I remember from my days at Newcastle United that young lads need progression to enhance their career and I feel we give them that at the club.

So, looking back, the club means everything to me and I'm eternally grateful to be having a role to play in this club's future. I enjoy the day-to-day banter with them, even if some of them were not born when we beat Liverpool on that magical night.

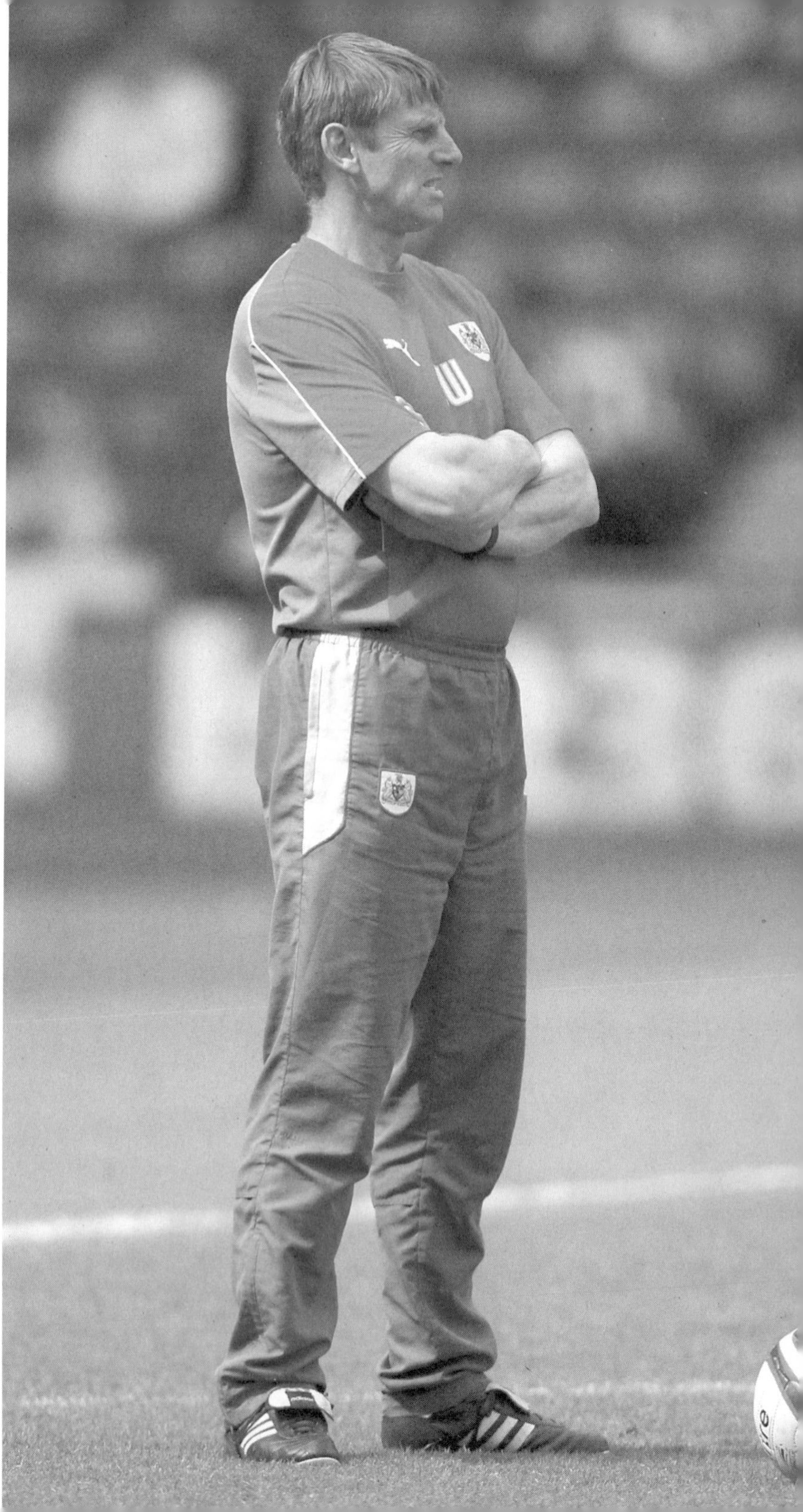

ALAN WALSH

Alan Walsh

Alan Walsh will always be regarded by the Bristol City fans as the best value-for-money player the club ever bought. With every game this quality striker played for City, it became apparent that the £18,000 City paid Darlington in 1984 was the steal of the century. This blond-haired north-easterner had skill, bravery, not to mention a killer left foot that tormented defenders throughout his time at Ashton Gate. He quickly became a fans' favourite, not only for his goals but his 'Walshy Shuffle', a combination of feints and step overs that mesmerised opponents and the crowd. Alan enjoyed success at the club, such as a famous trip to Wembley with City in the Freight Rover Final, as well as promotions and cup runs. He left city in 1989 to take up a lucrative offer in Turkish football with Besiktas, where he won a title and played European football. On his return three years later, he played for various clubs on a non-contract basis before dropping to non-league football with Taunton Town.

After a spell as community officer with Bristol Rovers, Alan returned to Ashton Gate in a coaching capacity under manager Gary Johnson. Today sees him out of the game full time but still living locally in the Portishead area of Bristol. Walsh will always be remembered as one of the club's great players who had a part in the rebirth of Bristol City during the eighties.

Bristol City 1 Doncaster Rovers 0
Football League Division Three
7 May 1988
Ashton Gate

Bristol City: Waugh, Llewellyn, Newman, Humphries, Pender, McClaren, Milne, Galliers, Gordon, Walsh, Neville. Sub: Jordan.

Goal: Gordon.

I could fill a whole book with goals and games that stick in my mind when I think about my time at Bristol City. I played my best football there and I have a great love for the club and the area, which is why I still live on the outskirts of Bristol today. I have so many games that come to mind, it's been really hard for me to pick one in particular, but it's also been really enjoyable looking back. I played in some big games for the club during my spell and they are still matches that get talked about even today. But let's start with how I came to arrive at Ashton Gate in the first place.

I was born in Hartlepool and always wanted to be a footballer. I had trials when I was a kid for Middlesbrough and Derby County but nothing happened. I just sort of resigned myself to continue playing but maybe I wasn't going to earn a living out of it. I got a job with a local brickmaking company and was playing men's football on a weekend, when I got a call from Middlesbrough who wanted to take me on a month's trial. I told my employers and they were great with me. Things went well and I was given a contract under manager John Neal.

I made three first-team appearances so I was over the moon when Neal informed me they had received an offer from Darlington for me. I was now 22 years old and I had a chance of regular first-team football, so I grabbed it. I spent six fantastic years at Darlington where I became the club's record scorer with 87 goals in 251 games. Two of those goals came in the 1982 season at Ashton Gate where Darlington drew 2–2 with City.

I had a good game and to be honest I always did against City. I remember City's then-manager Terry Cooper, who I knew from my playing days at Middlesbrough, saying to me after the game, 'You would love it here, Alan.' I didn't really think much of it until the following season when Darlington were away at Halifax and Terry was in the players' bar after the game with his assistant Clive Middlemass. Terry told me they wanted me at Bristol City and I told him I still had a year to go on my contract at the time. He said they would be making an offer but they couldn't afford a lot of money.

Anyway, months later my contract is up at Darlington and there's an offer of £18,000 from Bristol City which was a mile away from the £85,000 that Darlington wanted. So, as with things back then, it went to a tribunal. The tribunal was at Manchester City's Maine Road and the panel consisted of FA officials and Football League officials and ex-managers and an ex-player. I went in first and was asked why I wanted to go to Bristol City. I told them that City were now in a higher division, they had offered me a good package and, although I was Darlington's highest scorer, there was no improvement in the contract that was offered on their part. Then the Darlington manager Cyril Knowles went in with the chairman, and then Terry Cooper went in. After a couple of hours the decision was made and I became a Bristol City player and the fee was £18,000, which I was a bit embarrassed about, but you can imagine the delight on Terry's face.

I made my league debut against Wigan at Ashton Gate in a 2–0 win and got my first league goal two games later in a 2–2 draw with Swansea City. As I said, I have played in some great games for the clubs. I loved playing and scoring in any of the derby matches against Rovers. I really had no idea how intense those games would be and also how much it meant to the people of Bristol. Some of them were really torrid affairs where you had the responsibility of making sure the red half of the city went to work on a Monday with a smile on their faces. We also had the first ever Wembley appearance for Bristol City in 1986 where we beat Bolton 3–0 in the Freight Rover Final. I also remember the semi-final against Hereford and the scenes after the game were incredible. Getting to Wembley was a dream come true for the club and all our supporters. I think we took 30,000 fans that day and I'm sure if you ask any City player from that side what their greatest memory at the club is then to a man they would say that day. We followed it up the following year but lost to Mansfield on penalties which was heartbreaking for us. Terry Cooper was fantastic for me; he really allowed me to go and express myself, which was always part of my game.

And then we come to the 'Match of my Life'. I'm sure some fans will be surprised by my choice considering it's not one of the Wembley games or great cup runs, and not even a game I scored in, but it came about in what I always considered to be the best City team I ever played with, and also it was a season where we played in front of some massive crowds at Ashton Gate and I was voted player of the year. Although the season ended in disappointment it will always be at the forefront of my time at the club. The game was against Doncaster Rovers and it was the last game of the season. We needed to win to secure a place in the play-offs, which were a new thing for the league. Terry had invested in the squad, bringing in Steve Galliers, Steve McClaren and John Pender for around £300,000, which was a lot of money back then, but things had not really clicked for Terry and with about 11 games to go he moved upstairs and Joe Jordan took over as boss.

Going into the game we had only lost twice in Joe's 11 games since taking over and were really high in confidence coming off three wins on the trot. As with any sort of success Ashton Gate was full and really rocking. The supporters knew what we had to do and they were definitely going to be our twelfth man. Doncaster were a really tough outfit and a really young side with Brian Deane up front along with Steve Raffell and Rufus Brevett who had been part of the club's run to the FA Youth Cup Final that season. The first half was really nip and tuck with both sides having chances. Credit to them – their season was over but they never gave up and put us under real pressure at times. They had two golden chances, one when they stuck a ball high over the bar when it was easier to score, and another that I will never forget when their forward Chamberlain headed a ball that was going in, and I have no idea what

I was doing there, but I managed to head the ball off the line. I think that's why the game sticks in my mind so much to this day. I don't think I ever cleared a ball off the line, particularly in a game of this magnitude.

We went in 0–0 at half-time but the second half was much of the same until we got a breakthrough when Joe, who had come on as sub, was brought down and we got a penalty. Normally I would have been up there to take it but Colin Gordon, who was on loan from Reading, picked up the ball and took it. Incredibly he missed it and in a second we thought we had blown it. Thankfully with minutes left Colin got another chance and he slid into a 50/50 ball with the keeper and managed to poke it into the net. I was so pleased, especially for Colin as he had experienced the fine line between shattering failure and success within minutes. The crowd went crazy but we had to concentrate and see out the 90 minutes. I even had a left-foot shot well saved by the keeper in the very last minute. We looked at the referee and suddenly there was that whistle we were all waiting for. We had done it. I remember Joe punching the air and signalling to Terry Cooper in the stand who was on his feet. It was great that Joe acknowledged the work Terry had done in getting us there.

The end of the game was crazy. I think the whole of Ashton Gate emptied on to the pitch and I was trying to get into the tunnel, and when I did I was left in just my pants, socks and boots and the supporters would have had those off me had I not put up a fight. That's what I loved about that era – the fans were incredible and we had some fantastic crowds for a club that was in Division Three at the time. So the way the league was structured then was that Sunderland and Brighton had gone up leaving Walsall to play Notts County who had finished third and fourth and that left Bristol City, who had finished fifth, to play Sheffield United who had finished third from bottom in Division Two.

We went up to Bramall Lane full of confidence on the following Saturday. It was weird as we really didn't know how Sheffield United were going to be – were they on the floor about being in the play-offs or did they look at it as a bit of a reprieve? Anyway, we played really well and won 1–0 when I volleyed a cross from Steve McClaren into the net. The following Wednesday it was another full house at Ashton Gate that saw us win 1–0 through a Carl Shutt goal. We played Walsall home and away in the play-off final. I scored in the first game at home, but we were well beaten 3–1 which knocked the stuffing out of us. I remember Joe rallying us for the return leg and it worked as we ran out 2–0 winners. Remarkably we were level after extra time and had to take penalties to decide where the third game would take place. We lost 4–1 in the shoot-out and I had mine saved. We never turned up for the final game, losing 4–0. It was a day when Walsall forward David Kelly ran us ragged with a hat-trick. That run to the play-off final will always be in my memory when talking about my time at the club. There was also a famous League

Cup run that took us to the semi-final against Brian Clough's Nottingham Forest. It's a game that fans talk to me about a lot and, in particular, a shot I had late on that hit the inside of the post when the tie was poised at 0–0. Seconds later Forest scored and we were out.

There is nothing but affection whenever I think about my career at the club and I would have stayed had it not been for a massive financial offer from Besiktas of Turkey. They were managed by former Coventry City manager Gordon Milne and it came right out of the blue. I thought about it long and hard with my family and from a personal point of few they were offering good money, and from a career point of view I was a Third Division footballer being given the chance of European football and living in Istanbul of all places. So I signed and left City. In total I think my record was 284 games and 99 goals for the club which wasn't that bad. I had a few years in Turkey and I loved it. I won the league title twice and the cup once, as well as playing European football. On European nights the crowd were amazing. I knew it wasn't going to be a long-term thing so after my contract ended I came home.

I found it difficult to get a club and played for a few like Huddersfield Town, Cardiff City and Walsall, but it was all short-term stuff. In the end I decided to go non-league with Taunton Town and, can you believe it, I ended up playing at Wembley in the FA Trophy Final against Diss Town. The game ended in defeat for us but it was great to go back. After a few seasons in non-league I then got a call from my hometown club Hartlepool United asking if I would like to go up and play for a season. I couldn't turn it down although I was apprehensive as I had not played league football for a few years. I made my debut against Gillingham and we were awarded a penalty. So I picked the ball up and nobody wanted to take it, so I did and scored. It was my 200th goal in league football which was a fantastic end to my career.

After my contract finished I got a job with Bristol Rovers's community department before being asked back to Bristol City by manager Gary Johnson as part of his backroom staff. I always wanted to go into coaching; in fact, when I was playing at City, the chairman Des Williams used to tell me I would be a great youth team coach at the club. I really enjoyed working with Gary at the club and had some great times bringing the youngsters through. But as with football, when Gary left, so did I. Today I still live in the area and do some regional scouting for Stoke City part-time, which I love. But I would love to get back into the game on a full-time basis. I still go to Ashton Gate, usually for reunions with the lads from the 1980s. It's great to meet the fans and see some old faces. When I look back, it was a real privilege to have represented the club through some great times for us as players and for the fans. Let's hope there are some more good times to come in the future.

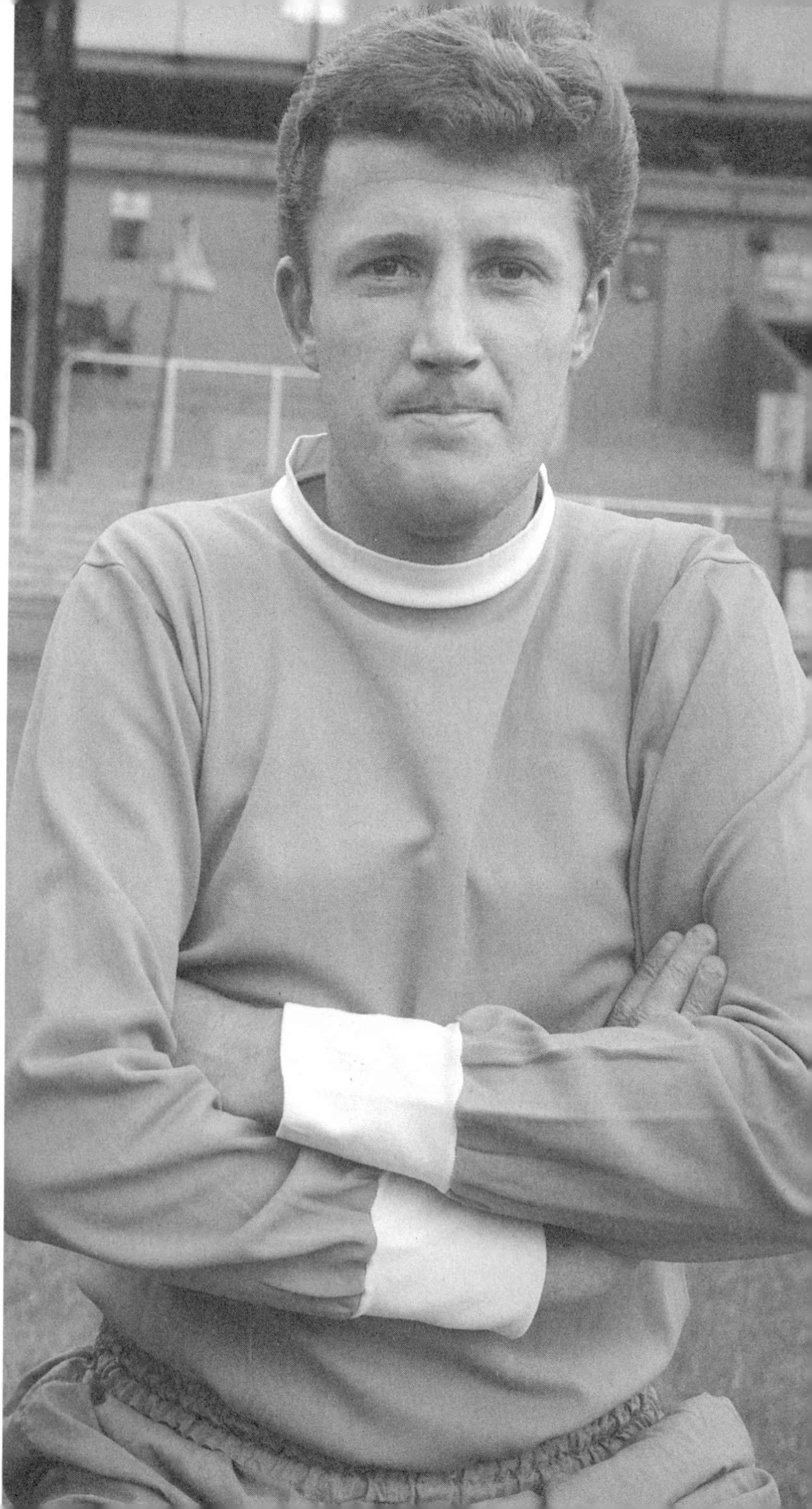

BOBBY WILLIAMS

Bobby 'Shadow' Williams

Bobby Williams learnt his trade as a youngster in the park under the shadow of Ashton Gate. This quick, skilful player had a knack for being in the right place at the right time, thus becoming the perfect foil in what would be regarded as one of Bristol City's greatest forward lines of Williams, Atyeo and Clark during the 1960s.

Williams was given the nickname of 'Shadow' by his older mates during those days in the park, as he always seemed to turn up hoping for a game when they were playing. The nickname was perfect for his career at City as he ghosted into the box on many occasions in his pursuit of goals. Sold by City to Rotherham United when at the very top of his game, Williams's departure never sat easy with City fans. Many of a certain age still shake their heads regarding the decision by the club. Spells at rivals Bristol Rovers, Ostend in Belgium and Reading have never stopped the affection that Bristol City fans have for this modest City great, something that is reciprocated on his part. In total he played 214 games and scored 82 goals in the red shirt. To many, Williams was the complete footballer whose vision for a pass would not be lost in today's game.

Halifax Town 2 Bristol City 5
Football League Division Three
27 April 1963
The Shay

Bristol City: Nicholls, Briggs, Thresher, Etheridge, Low, Waterhouse, Savino, Clark, Tait, Williams, Derrick.

Goals: Williams 4, Tait.

I am so grateful to be able to share my memories with Bristol City supporters through this book. Over the years I have played in some great games with some great players. The club are very special to me; they're not only my hometown club but the club that gave me a start in this wonderful game of football and I am so grateful to still be involved in the game today, albeit in a small capacity.

I know it's probably an old cliché but I really do love the club. I used to walk to Ashton Gate with my dad when I was a kid, and have endless memories such as the promotion team of 1955 with John Atyeo and Cyril Williams in the team. It was such an honour to end up playing with Big John. I always wanted to be a footballer. I used to play in the park opposite Ashton Gate and sometimes my older mates wouldn't let me play, but I never gave up, and in the end they would say 'Here he is again, our shadow' and that's where the nickname came from. My dad wrote to the club and asked if I could have a trial and sure enough they said yes, and that's how I ended up on the ground staff with the likes of Frank Jacobs and Jantzen Derrick.

They were great days on the ground staff. We had loads of jobs to do as well as trying to become better players. One of the jobs was to sweep the terraces on a Monday after a Saturday home game. We would run to the turnstile at the old East End as that's where the majority of fans rushing in late and usually drunk would drop their money as they paid. Obviously apprentices were treated different then. We cleaned boots, swept up and in the summer I even remember being sent out to paint red oxide paint on to the roof of the East End. It was crazy but you just got on with things. I don't think it would happen today, but it certainly kept us grounded, except when we were on the roof.

As I said, before I played with some great players, especially the likes of John Atyeo and Brian Clark, I remember John asking me when I joined what my ambitions were. I told him that I wanted to play in the first team, play alongside him and play for England. So two out of three wasn't a bad return. When it comes to remembering games, there are so many matches that come to mind. I remember scoring a cracker against rivals Bristol Rovers. I think it was a Gloucestershire Cup game at Ashton Gate. Rovers player Doug Hillard made a mistake and the ball dropped over his head and I volleyed it into the top corner. I think it was the best goal I ever scored for City. We won the game 4–1 in the end. Another game was against Southend United. We won 6–3 and I scored a hat-trick along with Barrie Meyer, who also got a hat-trick. It sticks in my mind as Barrie was dropped for the next game to make way for Brian Clark who was returning from injury. Barrie was certainly not happy with the decision. No disrespect to Barrie but Brian was such a great player up front for us that you really couldn't leave him out. He was a tremendously brave player. We had a great understanding, myself, John and Brian, so much so that we never practised anything in training – it just clicked on the day. I think that was when I played my best football alongside those two club legends.

So it comes to my match and I will always remember the game against Halifax Town, not because it was a massive game in terms of cups or titles but just because it was such a rollercoaster of a game to be involved in, plus the fact that I managed to score four goals. We were doing okay in Division Three at the time and Halifax were a mid-table club like ourselves. From a personal point of view I was scoring well and looking forward to getting on the scoresheet, so confidence was sky high. We travelled up north on the Friday and stayed at the Grand Hotel in Sheffield. Our manager Fred Ford gave us a team talk in the hotel and told us that the Yorkshire men could be a difficult team to break down. He reiterated this in the changing room before the match, also telling us to get the ball out wide to Jantzen whenever we could and for him to get the ball in for Brian and myself up front. We had a good side at the time and we could play a bit and also mix it with them if needed, especially with the likes of Briggs and Thresher at the back.

We started terribly and found ourselves two goals down after about 30 minutes; we just could not get going. I remember looking over to the bench and Fred Ford's face was like thunder. The crowd were making a lot of noise and for the first 40 minutes Halifax were playing some of their best football of the season. Then we got a chance and psychologically it made a massive difference to us. It was just before half-time. Alec Briggs won the ball and sent over a cross into the Halifax penalty area. The ball came back out and I hit it on the half-volley and from the moment I hit it I knew it was destined for the top corner. Within minutes the referee blew for half-time. We trudged off to the dressing room, hopefully thinking that the goal may have eased Fred's mood. This was not the case – he launched into us, calling us southern softies, effing and blinding about how these were real men up here and how they had taught us a real lesson, and if we continued to perform like this then we didn't deserve to wear the red shirt. He made no mention of our goal just before half-time; he just went on this amazing rant.

We went back for the second half with his words ringing in our ears, determined to get back in the game. Thankfully within minutes a cross from Jantzen fell at my feet and I struck the ball into the bottom corner to equalise. That goal really did turn the game on its head as Halifax turned to route one football hitting the ball up front as quick as they could, but our back four dealt with everything. For us, we started to play our normal passing game and we knew things would only get better for us as we had chance after chance. We then got another three goals in the space of about five minutes. Ray Savino and Jantzen Derrick were having a fantastic second half as they tore the Halifax full-backs apart. My hat-trick came as I managed to get on to a Jantzen cross. Then literally two minutes later Brian Clark shot and the keeper couldn't hold it and I stuck it in for my fourth. Our fifth goal came from Alex Tait minutes after that. The crowd, although not big, were in silence as the referee blew his whistle.

It's funny but I learnt years later that the centre-half who was marking me was Eric Harrison, who sadly passed away this year. Eric was the youth coach at Manchester United who was responsible for bringing the likes of David Beckham, the Neville brothers, Paul Scholes and Nicky Butt to United. I gave him a torrid time but to his credit he came over and shook my hand. I was on cloud nine as I had scored eight goals in three games and I will always remember Fred Ford as we came off. Fred stood at the edge of the pitch and shook hands with every one of us. As he did so he was saying, 'You showed them what real men are like. I knew you could do it. You taught these northern fools a thing or too.' I couldn't stop laughing; that was typical of Fred, and he forgot all about the half-time team talk. I even think he bought me a beer on the way home.

I continued to score goals every season for City, so it was a real shock two seasons later when Fred called me into his office and told me the club had accepted a bid from Rotherham United for me. I told him I wasn't interested in going but he and some of the directors put real pressure on me, telling me the club really could do with the £9,200 that Rotherham had bid, how it would be a good move for me and how I should go up and meet them. I had been in and out of the side for the last couple of games due to the emergence of the talented Gerry Sharpe, so as far as City were concerned it was a bit of a no-brainer for them as they would have a good fee for me and a ready-made replacement. I have to say that young Gerry was a smashing lad on and off the pitch. He even apologised to me for keeping me out of the team. I told him he was a very talented lad who would go on and have a great career. I was gutted to be going as the City teams were really playing some good football at that time and I wanted to be part of any success they might have had.

Anyway, I went up to Rotherham and met manager Jack Mansell, who seemed a really good bloke. Rotherham had a good side and were a division higher than City, but in reality my heart probably wasn't in it. Yet I signed, as I knew that Bristol City needed the money. I remember the fans were not happy when I left. I received some wonderful messages wishing me well and saying what an outrage it was that I was sold. It became very difficult for me when later on that year City won promotion to Division Two, as I would have loved to have been part of that. As I said, Rotherham had a good side, in particular a centre-forward called John Galley, who ended up at Bristol City due to a glowing recommendation from me. In hindsight, the move up north was a mistake. I did well up there but myself and my family couldn't wait to get back down south and as near to Bristol as I could. Looking back on my time there, I played 47 games and scored 12 goals. It wasn't a bad return and they were a good club with Jack Mansell in charge, who was a good bloke.

In my desperation to return south I ended up doing the worst thing a City player could possibly do and I signed for Bristol Rovers. Now, if I thought the Rotherham move was a mistake in terms of my career, moving across to the blue half of the city was a real disaster. I signed for Bert Tann's team and it was never really going to work. After a few games Bert pulled me aside and told me 'Listen, we don't go in for all that tippy-tap stuff here. We like to get the ball quickly up to Alfie Biggs and if he misses you just get what you can. If you want to play tippy-tappy, go and give Spurs a ring.' I think I knew then that my time at Rovers was nearing the end. I scored five goals in 29 games for the Pirates, but I did get a lot more goals in the reserves which was where I ended up.

I left on a free transfer and was on my way to Colchester United when I got a call from my old Rotherham manager Jack Mansell who asked if I would be interested in going to Reading, where he had become manager. So I signed for them. I spent two seasons with the Royals and I really loved the place. Like City, they are a club that has become close to my heart over the years. I enjoyed playing under Jack Mansell and in total I scored 20 goals in 64 games. I was getting older and started to think about what I might do when I finished the game, and coaching was something that really interested me, but I knew I had a few years left as a player. Reading gave me a free transfer at the end of my second season and, while I was wondering which direction to take, one of my Reading team-mates Ronnie Allen asked me if I would be interested in joining him in Belgium playing for AS Ostende. I was a bit dumbstruck to be honest as not many players from Britain went abroad to play in the early seventies. I wondered how it was going to work but the two clubs had worked it out that Ronnie and myself would train at Reading all week then fly out to Belgium on Friday nights, play the games on Saturdays and come home Sundays, which was perfect for my family as I didn't have to upheave them.

The standard of football was very skill-based with ball to feet, so it really suited my style. The standard was probably the equivalent of Division Three but I really enjoyed it for the couple of seasons, but I knew it wasn't going to last. I came back when my contract was finished and got a call from my old Bristol City team-mate Bobby Etheridge, who was manager at non-league Cheltenham Town. We agreed that I would play the remainder of the season for them and that suited me fine. So off to Cheltenham I went. I played the last six games of the season for them and what with my age now, I realised that league football was a thing of the past. In the summer I got a call from Weymouth and went down there for a few seasons.

Then one night, on my way home from a game away at Yeovil Town, I had a car accident in the fog that nearly killed me. I don't really remember much about it other than I think I fell asleep and hit a wall. I had a punctured lung, broken jaw, broken pelvis, smashed all my ribs and had some internal bleeding. The doctor told my family that only my fitness had saved me from death. I had a two-year recuperation that obviously took me away from football and any thoughts of what I would do next.

Then, whilst I was getting back on my feet, I got a call from the Reading boss Charlie Hurley who asked if I would be interested in coming back to the club as a youth team boss. I was overjoyed; it was just the shot in the arm I needed, and so I ended up youth team boss, then reserve boss doing the coaching that I had thought about doing years ago. I was youth team boss for around 25 years and I loved every minute of it. I have also been reserve team boss and there was a time that I thought about going for a manager's position. I wrote for a few but nothing happened.

Today I am still with Reading working as a scout and it's a job I love as it's still involved in the game. I go to matches to watch players and teams and write reports on the opposition. The role brings me back to Ashton Gate and a chance to meet up with some of my old pals. I get a great response from the supporters which is always nice. I'm shocked that there are fans who remember me. I was so pleased when I was asked to take part in this book as it's so lovely to be linked with Bristol City after all these years. I hope my game gave you as many memories as the club gave me.